SHEELAGH LEARY

Games For Kids

ANGUS & ROBERTSON PUBLISHERS

Illustrated by Mary Davy

To Gordon, always an enthusiastic games player

Acknowledgements

I would like to thank all the eager games players who have tried ideas with me: the children in standards 3 and 4 at Pinehaven School; my occupational therapy students; my own children and their friends. Thank you, too, Janene McDermott for being a most tolerant and helpful editor.

ANGUS & ROBERTSON PUBLISHERS

Unit 4, Eden Park, 31 Waterloo Road,
North Ryde, NSW, Australia 2113, and
16 Golden Square, London W1R 4BN,
United Kingdom

First published in New Zealand
by A.H. & A.W. Reed Ltd in 1984
First published in Australia
by Angus & Robertson Publishers in 1985
First published in the United Kingdom
by Angus & Robertson (UK) Ltd in 1985

Copyright © Sheelagh Leary, 1984

British Library
Cataloguing-in-publication data.
Leary, Sheelagh
   Games for kids.
   1. Games 2. Amusements
   I. Title
   790.1'922 GV1203

   ISBN 0-207-15210-1

Typeset by Computype New Zealand
Printed in the United Kingdom

Introduction

This book is the result of a number of years spent playing and working with children and finding out the games they like best. The games that follow are their choices for the most fun at a party, camp, sports day or on holiday. There are also plenty of games children like to play in pairs, on trips, or indoors in bad weather.

Keys to success

Whether the group is large or small, best results will come if the leader is thoroughly prepared. Have all the equipment you need to hand, be clear about the rules of each game and be sure that everyone is attending when you explain the game so you do not have to do it twice. Insist on fair play. Have plenty of games ready in case one is not a success. If a game obviously does not suit your group suggest they leave it and move on quickly to another game from your list of chosen activities.

Be cautious about games in which one person is made conspicuous. Although some of the following games are competitive, the emphasis is on team competition rather than rivalry between individuals.

A mixture of quiet and lively games is a good idea — plan for about one-third quiet games and two-thirds more vigorous activities. Also plan a schedule taking the energy levels of your group into account. With some groups I've found it hard to move back from lively games to quiet ones. Our school clubs group soon settled into a routine of 20 minutes of quiet games, followed by 20 minutes of lively games, then 20 minutes of vigorous games. The reverse would have been impossible! For a party, plan some quieter games after the food interval.

In the introductions to the various sections there are notes on suggested age groups, numbers of players, playing times and so on. These, of course, are flexible. If enthusiasm wanes before time's up don't bother to finish the game. Just say, "We'll leave it now," and move on to another. It all depends so much on the occasion and who is prepared to let their hair down and frolic. When the age range is mixed, adults will enjoy many of the games, too.

When any special equipment is needed, whether the game is intended for a larger number or older or younger group of players, whether the game depends on luck or skill and why this is significant are noted prominently above each game.

After reading the introductions you should be able to pick a varied selection of games from the different sections to suit any age group or any occasion.

Sheelagh Leary

Getting started, choosing teams

Instead of introducing children to each other at the beginning of a party, play group or games session, start by playing greeting games. Players will quickly learn each others' names and get to know each other through these games.

The following games are good conversation starters. Any number of players can join in. They can be played for any length of time, but eight to 10 minutes is a good guide.

Most five-year-olds could manage to play *Introductions*. The other games are suitable for eight-year-olds and older children.

Not a great deal of preparation is needed; but, if you have the time, extra preparation will make for a more interesting start to your games session. The equipment required is shown above the various games.

Teams

Here are some ways of dividing players into teams.

Numbering off
Probably the easiest way of choosing teams is to number off players around the group. This mixes them up randomly. But sometimes random mixing may not be the ideal approach. Perhaps players who know each other would be better grouped together?

Card sets
Give out Happy Families cards and ask the players to match themselves and assemble in teams of four.

For larger groups use ordinary playing cards. Decide how many people will be in each team and give out that number of cards from each suit (for example, for six players in each team give out the ace to six from each suit). The first game could be a race for all players to line up in order in various suits.

Songsters

A variation on the above game is to give out slips of paper on which are written lines of well-known songs like *Rule Britannia* and *Yellow Submarine*. Ask the players to find the rest of their song then sing themselves to all the other players.

Choosing starters

Here are some traditional ways of deciding which teams start the play.
* Flip a coin, once or take the best of three.
* Hand over hand up a broomstick — the team leaders take turns to grasp a broom handle with one hand placed close above the previous player's hand. The team whose leader grasps the top part of the handle starts.
* Roll one or more dice.
* Cut a pack of cards.
* Empty a box of matches on a table and let the players or leaders take turns to pick them up. Whoever picks up the last match starts.

Introductions

Seat the players in a circle and pick one to begin the game. That player introduces themselves with a word of description and their name (for example, "Jolly Janet"). Each player in turn lists the names of the previous players before introducing themselves (for example, "Jolly Janet, Laughing Louise, Joking John . . . and I'm Marvellous Michael").

Sealed orders

Equipment prepared instruction slips

Write out a secret assignment for each player and hand out the assignments as they arrive. Choose tasks that suit the mood of the occasion and the ages of the participants. Some suggestions: find Stuart Simpson and introduce him to Neil Norton and Angela Sutherland; find out the names of everyone's pets; make a list of everyone's favourite puddings or pet hates.

Who am I?

Equipment prepared cards

Make a card for each player bearing the name of a famous person or character (perhaps a sports figure, politician, nursery rhyme character or cartoon character). Pin a card on the back of every player without letting them see the name they are given. Each player must try to discover who they are by asking only *one* question of every other player.

Partners

Equipment prepared cards

In this game, every player is given a prepared card which makes a pair with a card held by another player. The pair might be a riddle and its answer, or a joke and its response (for example, "What do you get when you cross an elephant with a mouse?" Written on the paired card is the response, "Huge holes in the skirting board"). It might be the name of an animal and its young (for example, "swan" and "cygnet", "goat" and "kid" — in this case players can make the noise the animal makes to pair up). Or it might be the name of a book and its author, or two words that go together (for example, "foot" and "ball").

Clumps games

In the games in this section the players huddle together in clumps while they try to guess the answers.

No equipment is needed for Act and guess or Talk and guess. For the other games you will need to spend a little time in advance making up lists of mystery objects to be guessed and/or collecting various items. The things you will need are listed below.

These games generally last for at least five minutes each. Recommended age levels are listed beside each game. They can all be played by two or more people (even an adult and one child), but groups of four or five are best.

Act and guess

Age 5–adult

The aim of this acting game is to guess the identity of a mystery object, animal or person, or to guess a location or activity that is being acted out.

One person may choose the subject to be guessed, with everyone firing questions at him or her until the answer is found. Alternatively, the game may be organised so that one player or a small group question all the others who have chosen the mystery subject. In this case, the player or players trying to guess the mystery should put one question to each actor in turn.

If you want to limit the guessing time, make a rule that only 20 questions may be asked. If the guessers find out the answer before they have used up their questions, they are the winners. If the subject is still a mystery after 20 questions have been asked, the actor(s) has won and must then reveal the answer. Sometimes it will be a good idea to work out who will choose the mystery in a predetermined order. Age is a good criterion for this.

Here are some ideas to start the game. Remember to demonstrate each of them.

"Where am I?" Answer: "Trying to hide in a box."

"What am I?" Answer: "A duck egg."

"Who am I?" Answer: "Spiderman."

"What am I doing?" Answer: "Washing an elephant."

"What animal am I?" Answer: "A rabbit."

"What is it?" (In this case, give a clue — animal, vegetable or mineral.) Answer: "A crayon."

Very young players can cope with acting and guessing "Where am I?" and "What animal am I?"

Listen and guess

Age 3–20
Equipment sound-making items

Listen and guess is played by making a selection of noises to be guessed from behind a barricade or around a corner so you will not be seen. Some examples: brushing shoes, striking a match, bouncing a ball, pouring rice into a pan, cutting paper, tearing a piece of material, breaking a carrot.

Talk and guess

Age 6–adult, depending on topic

Arrange the sequence and grouping of players for this game as described for Act and guess above.

In this game the mystery is a word — a noun, a verb or an adverb. Decide which it will be at the beginning of each round. The players question whoever has chosen the word. If it is a noun or verb, the person replies by talking about the mystery object or activity, substituting the word "teapot" for the mystery word whenever it arises.

For instance, let's say the word is "bicycle". In answer to a question concerning the use of the mystery object, the person who has chosen the word might say, "I teapot my way to school every day." This is a simple example, but the game may be made much more complex by choosing words with two meanings, such as "box", "saw", "pear or pair".

If the word is an adverb, the player who has chosen it must reply to the questioners in the manner described by the adverb — for example, slowly, grandly, skittishly. The other players must guess the word from the tone and manner of the reply.

Draw and guess

Age 8–adult
Equipment pencil and paper for each group
                   prepared list of objects to be guessed

Divide the players into two or more small groups. Ask each group to choose one person who will go up to the organiser and collect a pencil, paper and the first topic to draw. These players must then hurry back to their groups and draw what they have been told without saying a word (apart from "yes" or "no"), without writing anything or indicating the number of letters. As soon as another group member identifies the drawing it is their turn to rush up to the organiser for the next subject. The winning group is the one that completes guessing all the subjects first.

The subjects must be suited to the ages of the players. For instance, give eight to 10-year-olds simple topics like a car,

Tower Bridge or a flower. Older players and adults could try complex subjects like porridge, lino, hope, a stolen kiss. The most difficult we've tried was peaceful coexistence. With older players make sure they get the exact wording of the original clue.

Cut and guess

Age 6–adult
Equipment scissors and paper

This is a variation of Draw and guess. The players cut out silhouettes of the subjects to be guessed. Some examples: a car, a slipper, a tortoise, sunglasses, grass. Cutting out shapes is more difficult than drawing them, so the subjects can be simpler than those used in Draw and guess.

Senses

Age 5–20
Equipment bag of finger foods

For a game of guessing tastes, try a blindman's lunch. Prepare a bag of titbits in advance. Ask the players to close their eyes and open their mouths, and pop something in to be munched and identified. Some examples: raisins, pieces of celery, uncooked macaroni, bean sprouts.

Lists

Here is a selection of alphabet games you can play with no equipment. Allow at least five minutes for each game. Before each game are suggested age levels and numbers of players.

Aunty's alphabet amble

Age 5–20
No of players 3 or more

For this alphabet and memory game everyone sits in a row or circle and one player is chosen to start the game.

Player 1 begins by saying, "My aunt went to Acton Town and she took . . . an alligator." The first item must have the initial letter "a", the second "b" and so on. So Player 2 might say, "My aunt went to Acton Town and she took . . . an alligator and a balloon." Each succeeding player must name in order all the items already mentioned before adding their own suggestion. Players are out if they forget any of the luggage.

By the time the letter "h" comes up, the list of "my aunt's" belongings the players must remember and recite before they add their own might be: an *a*lligator, a *b*alloon, a *c*rayon, a *d*uck, an *e*gg, a *f*ossil and a *g*olden retriever.

Players can decide whether their "aunt" is a specialist and would take only foodstuffs, or flowers, or that "aunt" might be going on a trip to collect animals for a zoo or making a list of placenames visited. The same rule of taking turns to add an item with the correct initial letter applies.

Action aunts

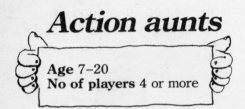

Age 7–20
No of players 4 or more

This game is similar to the previous one, but instead of taking luggage "aunt" performs an action as she goes. For instance:

Player 1. "My aunt went to town waving all the way." (Everyone must wave.)
Player 2. "My aunt went to town waving and nodding her head all the way." (Everyone must wave and nod their heads.)

The game continues until it is impossible to have "aunt" doing anything else.

Next town

Age 10–20
No of players 2 or more

In this game each word must begin with the last letter of the previous word on the list.

The words must be the names of towns, but let younger players add the names of countries or counties as well.

Player 1 begins by naming a town or city, perhaps "Manchester". Player 2 must then think of a town or city beginning with "r", perhaps "Rye". Player 3's town must begin with the letter "e", and so on. Players who are completely stumped drop out.

Animal necklaces

Age 7–10 minimum
No of players 2 or more

The object of this game, a variation of the above game, is for players to think up strings of animal names, each of which begins with the last letter of the previous name. Choose a name to begin the game and set a time limit of five minutes. The winner is the player with the longest string of names. (For example, hors*e*, *e*lephan*t*, *t*ige*r*, *r*acoon and so on.)

"Necklaces" can also be played using names of people or food. It can be a pencil and paper game rather than a talking game, too.

Minister's cat

Age 7–20
No of players 2 or more

This is another alphabet game, in which a list of adjectives, each beginning with succeeding letters of the alphabet or all with the same initial letter, is formed. The adjectives can be insulting or complimentary, and each player adds one to the chain begun by the previous players.

It might go like this:
"The minister's cat is *a*bsurd, *b*ald, *c*razy, *d*andruffy, *e*mpty-headed . . ." or "The minister's cat is *p*ompous, *p*lump, *p*itiful, *p*imply . . . ."

You have a face

Age 7–20
No of players 2 or more

This is a variation of the previous game, in which players address their adjectives to the face of the next player.

For instance:

Player 1: "You have a face."

Player 2: "What kind of face?"

Player 1 then starts the demoralising list. The insulted person then has the satisfaction of continuing the game with the next player and adding another insulting adjective to the list.

Why?

Age 7–20
No of players 4 or more

This is another game of taking things on a trip, but this time players don't have to worry about alphabetical order. It starts like this:

Player 1 (the organiser): "Each player must repeat what I say, but must choose a different item to take. I went on a trip and I took a banana."

Player 2: "I went on a trip and I took my hat."

Player 3: "I went on a trip and I took my umbrella."

When everyone has had a turn Player 1 says: "Repeat what I say again, but when I say 'banana' you must substitute the item you said in the first round. I went on a trip and took a banana to eat."

Player 2: "I went on a trip and took my hat to eat."

Player 3: "I went on a trip and took my umbrella to eat."

The organiser can decide to take whatever he or she likes for whatever purpose. One round is all that works for this game.

Quizzes and guessing games

Here is a small selection of quizzes for individual players or small teams. Allow five to 10 minutes for each game. Unless stated otherwise, each player will need a pencil and paper.

Suitable age levels have been suggested above each game. As a rough guide on how difficult to make a quiz, most players need to get more than half the answers correct to find the game fun.

If these games are especially enjoyed, invent more quizzes of your own. Topics may include book titles, poems, nursery rhymes and questions such as who invented X, who was the first person to do X, where does X come from or where do people do X (everyday actions or foreign customs)?

Guess and check

Age 8–15
Equipment tape measures
prepared list of items (as suggested below)

The things to aim for in this game are speed, good estimates and accurate checking. Each player or team should work out and write down their guess for each item, then measure or count to check their accuracy. Where the players are working in teams, the checking work should be shared. Award points for speed, good guesses and accurate checking.

Some items to guess are the length of the room, the number of peas in a jar, the number of floor-boards in the room, the length of a ball of string, the number of potato crisps in a packet, the number of pips in an apple, and so on.

Wood, cotton, plastic

Age 9–12

Ask each player or team to list as many things in the room as they can under the categories in the heading. Give them a time-limit of five minutes. Add metal, fabric and paper to the list of categories if you like.

Fiction facts

Age 10–20
Equipment a paperback book for each player or team

Give each player or team a similar book and tell them to take a good look at it so they can answer questions about it afterwards. Some suggested questions for the quiz: Who wrote it? Who published it? Where? How long ago? Was it reprinted? Are there any acknowledgements? What is the starting page number? What is the last page number? How many chapters? Does it have a dedication? How many lines are there to each page?

Travelling

Age 11–16
Equipment atlas

Ask each player or team to imagine themselves travelling in one direction and to list all the towns and cities they can think of. Give one point for each town listed in its correct order, and take away one point for any listed out of sequence. For example travelling north from London the list might include Watford, St Albans, Luton, Milton Keynes and so on.

Stunts

All these stunts are physical. Some of them most people will find pretty hard, but others will be able to do them fairly easily. Try them out with your friends and see how supple you are.

Stand-up stunt

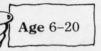

Age 6–20

Lie on the floor on your stomach with your arms folded behind your back. Now try to get up without moving your arms!

Circles

Age 6–teenagers

Stand on your left leg and swing the right leg in a clockwise circle. Hold your right arm out and swing it in anticlockwise circles at the same time.

Coin challenge

Age 6–20

Mark a toe line on the floor. The object of this stunt is to *place* a coin as far away from the line as possible without falling over. Players stand on the toe line and are allowed to place one hand on the floor beyond the line while placing (not throwing or flipping) the coin as far away as possible. For their turn to count, the player must return to the standing position in one movement after placing the coin, without putting the hand that held the coin on the ground.

Alternative: Allow the supporting hand to be moved as much as the player wants, but only that hand may be used to support the player while returning to the standing position.

Chimneying

Age 7–11 (this stunt works only for children of fairly small size)
Equipment a door frame

For this stunt, "walk" or "chimney" up a door frame with your bare feet against one side and your hands against the other, as illustrated.

Pick up money

Age 6–20
Equipment a coin or matchbox

Stand with your heels against a wall and attempt to pick up a coin or matchbox placed one metre away from you, *without* lifting your heels away from the wall.

Pick up the pencil

Age 6–20

Kneel down and put your elbows against your knees with your palms out flat on the floor. Place a pencil at your fingertips. Now clasp your hands behind your back and try to pick up the pencil with your teeth.

Broomstick challenge

Age 8–20 (this stunt is not suitable for proving that life begins at 40. Fourteen is much more like it!)
Equipment a broom handle or stout stick about 2 metres long

Begin by holding the stick behind your back in both hands with your palms facing downwards and thumbs to the front. Without altering your grip at any stage (although you can let your hands *slide* along the stick), lift the stick over your head to the front of your body, lift your right leg up and put it around your right arm and through to the *inside* of the space between the stick and your body. Now pass your left hand over your head and back and step out of the stick.

Pencil and paper games

These games can be played by individuals or small groups working together. Some can be enjoyed by one person on their own. Unless noted otherwise, all players will need a pencil and paper.

These pencil and paper games usually last about five minutes, although *Vowels are out* is suitable for a 10-minute game. Set a time limit before you start, or call "Time's up" as soon as most groups are doing more thinking than writing.

For some of these games you will have to prepare word lists. Instead of making up one long list, plan for a short game and have a second list of words ready if the players want to continue.

The success of all these games depends on the players' level of skill, so monitor the subjects accordingly and select games suitable for the age level of the players.

How many?

Age 6–15

The object of this game is to come up with the longest list. Give each player a pencil and paper and ask them to write down as many examples of the subject as they can think of in three or five minutes. Some ideas: names of birds, cars, planes, fruit, vegetables, flowers, trees, drinks, puddings, boys' names, girls' names, compound words.

Vary the game by specifying a starting letter and decreasing the time allowed (for instance, "How many vegetables starting with "c" can you think of in one minute?").

Another variation is to ask for words beginning with letter pairs, such as "fl", "st", "sm", "ch" and so on. Some more difficult word beginnings are "dis", "un", "in" and "for". "Imp", "pro" and "con" are harder still.

Word box

Age 8–15

Ask each player to draw a naughts and crosses grid (3 x 3 squares) and then to take turns calling out letters of the alphabet. As a letter is called each player writes it somewhere on their grid. When nine letters have been called, the players count the number of words they have made. Words can run across the grid horizontally, vertically and diagonally.

A more difficult version of this game is played on a 4 x 4- or 5 x 5-letter grid.

Unscramble

Age 8–20
Equipment prepared lists of words

Make a list for each player of 10 to 20 words with the letters in the wrong order. Then start a race to sort them out. Begin with four-letter words and progress to larger words. The game may be made easier by choosing words that can be categorised (for instance, names of towns, names of fruit, girls' names and so on).

For a more difficult version of this game leave out one of the letters in each word.

Fill-ins

Age 6–10
Equipment prepared word lists

Choose 10 to 20 four-letter words. Give the players the first and last letters of each, or the two middle letters and ask them to complete the words using any letters that fit and make sense. The winner is the player who finishes first.

For older players, choose five-letter words.

Word pyramids

Choose a word to begin the game (one of the players' names is a good idea). Each player writes the letters in the word, well spread out, at the top of a piece of paper. Under each letter they must write a two-letter word beginning with that letter of the alphabet. Below that they must write a three-letter word beginning with the letter at the head of the column, then a four-letter word, and so on. Players need not complete one line before going on to the next.

Score 2 points for all two-letter words, 3 for three-letter words, and so on.

Definitions

Challenge the players to write definitions of some everyday words. The winning descriptions are those closest to the dictionary definitions. Use a dictionary suited to the age group of the players and check the definitions before the game. Mark the pages with strips of paper so they may be easily found. Some good examples to start with are "car", "box", "table" and "book".

Missing words

Select fairly well-known lines from advertisements, poems, popular sayings or proverbs. Write each one on a number of cards to suit the number of players, leaving out several words. The winner is the first to fill in all the missing words.

Telegram

Each player must work out a telegram message using the letters of a name they have chosen as the initial letters of each word in the telegram. They must be in the right order.

For example, if the word chosen is "Harold" the message might read: "Have Arrow, Require Optician. Lying Down." (King Harold was shot in the eye at the Battle of Hastings in 1066.) As another example, the word "Starlight" might result in the following message: "Stopped to arrest rogue. Learned imminent grand highway theft."

Bridges (acrostics)

Age 10–adult

Choose a word and write it down one side of a piece of paper, then backwards down the other side. The aim of the game is to find words to bridge the gaps between the pairs of letters. Players win a point for every letter they use, so the longer the words the better.

Doubles

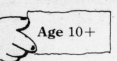

Age 10+

Each player writes the alphabet down one side of a piece of paper then, beside as many letters as possible, writes words containing two of that letter together. For instance, Aaron, beside A, bubble beside B, accept beside C and so on. It will be easier if proper names are allowed. Score a bonus for a, h, i, j, q, u, v, w, x, y and z, or score three points for words containing these difficult letters together and one point if the word contains two of the letter separated.

Beside X you may have to use something like "ex-xylophone player", or "ex-x-ray man".

Stepwords

This game starts with a pair of words with the same number of
letters. The object of the game is to progress from the first word to
the paired word in a series of steps in which only one letter is
changed each time. For example, "dog" may be changed to "cat" by
first substituting the "g" with a "t" (dot), then the "d" with a "c"
(cot), then the "o" with an "a" (cat). There are four steps — dog,
dot, cot, cat. The winner is the player with the smallest number of
steps. Some good examples to try are "bed" to "cot", "black" to
"white", "slow" to "fast" and "rich" to "poor".

Categories

Choose a word and write it across the top of a piece of paper, with
the letters well spread out. Down the side of the page list a number
of categories. Let the children choose whatever categories they want
— car makes, television stars, book characters, for instance. The
object of the game is for each team or player to fill in the spaces
under the letters with words that fit the category and begin with the
letter above. Let teams or players race each other, or everyone can
work together just for the fun of solving the puzzle.

Ghosts

This is a word game played verbally. One player thinks of a letter and
then each player in turn adds a letter (at either end). The aim is to
avoid being the player who completes a word. When adding a letter
the player must have a word in mind to reveal if he or she is
challenged.

Beetle drive

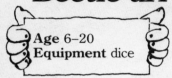

Age 6–20
Equipment dice

Beetle playing may be played by two players, or by pairs of players working together against other pairs. A tournament or beetle drive is fun for a large number of players. Play starts in pairs, with winning pairs playing other winning pairs and keeping note of their total number of wins until one pair of players is dubbed the final winner.

The object of the game is to be the first player or pair to draw a complete beetle. The throw of a dice governs when players may start and add parts to their picture. Turns are taken to throw the dice.

A six must be thrown to start and allows that player or pair to draw the body. Players must throw a five for a head, a four for each antenna, a three for a tail, a two for each eye and a one for each leg. The first player or pair to finish their picture wins.

An alternative to this game is Aeroplanes, in which players draw an aeroplane instead of a beetle. They must throw a one for the body, a two for the wings, a three for the tail wings, a four for the tail upright, a five for each jet (or propeller) and a six for the pilot's window.

Longest word

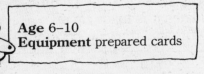

Age 8–20

Ask the players to write the longest word they can think of beginning with a certain letter of the alphabet. Then ask them to write down the longest word they can think of which includes a pair of letters such as b and d, or m and n. Score the game according to the word length.

Age 6–10
Equipment prepared cards

An alternative, for younger players, is to make letter cards and hold them up in turn. Give the card to the first player, who says a word beginning with the letter being displayed. You may need many cards for some letters if everyone knows words beginning with those letters. Progress to holding up two cards showing common word beginnings, such as "ch", "sh" and "st". You can vary the game by asking players for names (birds, fruit, vegetables and so on) beginning with the letters being held up.

Anagrams

Age 8–20

Choose several words and ask the players to think of as many other words as possible, using all the letters in the original word. Some good words to begin with are "post" (which can be made into "spot", "pots", "tops" and so on), "dear", "arts", "tears", "asleep", "seat" and "seal".

Age 11–adult

A more difficult variation of this game is progressive anagrams, in which the letters are rearranged and another letter is added in each step to make progressively larger words (for example, "as", "sap", "pals", "lapse", "please").

What was that?

Age 8–adult
Equipment 2–4 prepared drawings

At the beginning of this game one person from the group of players is given a drawing, which he or she takes back to the group and describes to the other players, without letting them see it. Each member of the group must try to draw what is described. The person describing the drawing may not tell the subject of the picture; he or she may describe only the shapes and lines it is made up of. The player whose effort looks most like the original drawing becomes the describer in the next round of the game.

Gulargambone

Age 8–20

In this word game each player must see how many words he or she can make from the letters in the word "Gulargambone". Each letter may be used only the number of times it appears in the basic word, unless you want the contest to be really complex, but the letters can be used to make as many new words as the player can think of. Score by giving a point for each word or a point for each letter in each new word, so that long words score more than short ones. If you like, add "s" to the end of each word to increase the possible score greatly. An alternative way of comparing results is to read out the list, while each player crosses off words duplicated on his or her list. However, with this method the scores never seem so grand.

For a shorter game, try the word "outing", or see who is the first to get 10 or 20 words from the basic word.

Vowels are out

Age 12–20

This may be a team game or a game for individual players. The object of the game is to compose sentences without using vowels — a, e, i, o, u. The first one may be a sentence without the letter "e". Choose the "best sentence" by common consent. Delete other letters, or combinations of letters, until the game is too difficult to be continued.

Constantinople

Age 8–20

In this game players try to make as many words as possible beginning with the letter C from the letters in Constantinople. Allow a time limit of two minutes.

Party games

Before deciding which games to play, think of a theme for the party. This will give you plenty of ideas for things like invitations, decorations and food, and the games will be easier to choose.

An "outer space" party might have twenty-first century decorations and a cake shaped like a spaceship. A "pink" party would be pretty, whereas a "fisherman's" party suggests a very different scene. Let imagination have free rein and include the children in preparations.

Invitations

Why not make your own and begin the party theme with the invitations? Try cutting cards into suitable shapes for your theme or fold them in such a way that they are interesting to take out of the envelope. The words of the invitation could be mixed up to form a puzzle. If you do this be sure the results will not be ambiguous, especially concerning the time and date of the party and the street number of your house.

Matchbox invitation
This is an idea which involves guests or members before they arrive. Ideally, collect enough empty matchboxes for everyone who is to be invited and send your message of invitation folded up inside it.

On the message tell those invited that there will be a prize for the person who brings the matchbox filled with the largest number of different items. The guests should arrive with numbered lists of the contents of their matchboxes. The list might read something like this: one tea leaf, one dog hair, one grain of salt, and so on. A hundred items can easily be squeezed in!

The winner receives a matchbox containing as many prize items as you have been able to fit into it. It might contain any of these: a coin, a rubber, a sweet, a balloon, a pencil sharpener.

Decorations

Apart from the ideas you have to fit your theme, the party room or garden may be decorated with streamers, balloons, flowers and so on. Here are some ideas for room and table decorations.
* Use a felt-tipped pen to draw faces or pictures on balloons.
* Make snowflake place mats by folding squares of paper several times and cutting out small shapes.
* Make your own place markers to fit the theme of the party.
* Coloured serviettes folded in a fancy way will make the table look good.
* Frost the rims of drinking glasses by dipping them into a shallow dish of lemon juice, then into sugar. Allow one hour for these to dry.
* Decorate straws by cutting circles of thin cardboard to fit over them, then colour and decorate the circles.
* Make an unusual trimming for the cake.
* Using thin card and lengths of hat or shirring elastic, make masks (leaving the eyes and mouth uncovered, of course!)
* Paper hats can be made by sewing or glueing decorations onto crepe paper, then joining the edges to fit around a child's head.

Food

Food poses some problems, like how much to make and what is "in". Be guided by suggestions from the children. Generally, it is sensible to make all the items small to avoid waste. Have all the food on view from the beginning of the party so the children can plan for their own appetite. Sweets or goodies that appear later may tempt some beyond reasonable limits. A table laid outdoors can reduce mess.

For children over seven years of age "do-it-yourself" food can be fun. Put out a selection of delicacies so they can make their own sundae, hamburger, pancake filling or pizza topping.

Prizes, or take-home gifts

If you want to award small prizes to the winners of some of the games or give a little gift to each guest as a party souvenir, here are some ideas: a liquorice stick, a felt pen from a pack, a ribbon, fancy hair clips, a ruler, chalks, crayons, marbles, stamps, Sellotape, a small notebook.

Now for the games!

Those played at the beginning and end of a party are especially important. The first few games set the style of the party, but there is a problem in that guests may not all arrive at once. I recommend some of the mind-reading and *What's the catch?* games for this period. They are mostly brief and newcomers can join in easily. For the same reason they can be useful at the end of the party when guests are leaving.

When everyone has arrived, start with the greeting and clumps games at the beginning of the book. Then move on to the games in this section. Lists of equipment, numbers of players and recommended age groups are noted before each game. These games generally last from five to 15 minutes, although some (such as table soccer) can go on a lot longer.

On page 56 is a reminder list of traditional party games familiar to most people.

Plan a clear ending to the party, when prizes will be announced and everybody will be involved in a group activity such as singing. After this point have ready a selection of games that can be played by small groups or any number of players except large teams. This way your party will end in style.

Who's who?

Age 5–adults in some settings
No of players 6 or more
Equipment a baby photograph of each guest or player
pencils and paper

Ask your guests to bring a photo of themselves as a baby and explain that these are not to be shown around before the party. Line up the photos on the wall or table, leaving them in place for the length of the party, and see whether everyone can identify who's who.

How green you are

Age with older leaders, tiny children can join in (4+)
No of players 3 or more

One person is chosen to leave the room while the others choose an object or action for him or her to hunt for or perform. The person who went out then returns and tries to discover the chosen object or action, guided by the singing of the other players. When the player is "cold" they sing very, very quietly. When the player is "hot", or close to the object or making an action similar to the correct one, they sing very loudly. The tune is "Old Lang Syne" and the words are "How green you are" sung over and over again.

Marble race

Age 4–15, depending on the complexity of the target
No of players 2 or more
Equipment cardboard box
              scissors
              pen
              marbles

This is a quiet game which involves some preparation. You will need a goal made from a cardboard grocery box.

Cut off the top and part of the sides of the box as shown, then cut different-shaped slots in the front and label them.

Give each player five marbles (or one marble to be used for five turns) and mark the place where they are to be shot from.

Watch the holes the marbles go through and add together the scores on the front of the box.

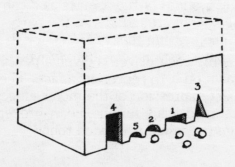

Where is Tom Thumb hiding?

Age 5–12
No of players 2 or more

Each player has a turn choosing a place in the room the right size for an imaginary Tom Thumb to hide. Everyone else tries to guess where it is.

Bird, beast, fish

Age 6–12
No of players 6 or more
Equipment ball

Everyone forms a circle or a line and the leader throws a ball to players in any order, calling out "Bird", "Beast" or "Fish" as the ball is thrown. Whoever catches the ball each time throws it back, calling out the name of a bird, beast or fish — whichever the thrower called to them. No creature may be called twice, and players must respond before the leader can say "Bird, beast, fish" three times.

Another version of this game is to call out a letter and the catcher must call a name (animal, food) starting with that letter.

Moods

Age 6–12
No of players 4 or more
Equipment pencils and paper

In each round of this game each player is given a pencil and sheet of paper with a circle drawn on it to represent a face. The object of the game is to draw the best expression of the mood suggested for each round. Some examples: mad, glad, furious, heart-broken.

Let the players judge the winners of each round.

Hidden objects

Age 6–adult (this is also a good game for an adult party when the guests are not keen on more organised "games")
No of players 4 or more
Equipment various hidden items (see below)
duplicates of the hidden things, or a list of them
pencils and paper

The purpose of this game is to find hidden objects which are actually visible without anything being moved but are carefully camouflaged.

Collect an assortment of things and either have duplicates of them for players to look at or make a list for everyone to copy before they start looking. Include a few really difficult ones. For older children these could be a word in a book title in your bookshelf, an object in a picture on the wall or a coloured stamp stuck onto a background of the same colour. Each player secretly ticks items off their list as they find them.

A friend had a potato on his list. It proved very difficult to find. The potato had been trimmed to the size of the bobbles on his old-fashioned blinds and had been carefully sewn into place where one was missing.

Leave the objects in place for the duration of the party.

Mouse

Age 6–12
No of players 6 or more
Equipment blindfold — perhaps a large paper bag

This is a game to be played once the party is in full swing. If it is played too near the beginning, players may not know each other's names or recognise their voices.

All players except one form a ring and walk around and around. One player is blindfolded and asked to stand in the centre of the circle. The blindfolded player must point to someone in the ring and say, "Squeak to me." The players forming the ring immediately stop moving and the person who was pointed to must pretend to be a mouse and squeak to the blindfolded player. If the player in the centre guesses who is squeaking, they change places.

Charades

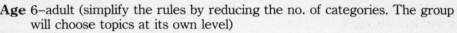

Age 6–adult (simplify the rules by reducing the no. of categories. The group will choose topics at its own level)
Time 2-10 minutes per round
Equipment some prepared topics as examples

In charades one player silently acts out things for the other players to guess. Topics are usually words, well-known phrases or book, film, song or television series titles.

The following conventional signs are used as clues. Check that all players are familiar with them before the game starts.

Book title: two hands held palms upwards to indicate an open book.
Film title: mime winding a handle to indicate a movie camera.
Song title: hold a make-believe microphone.
Television series: draw a box in the air.

The number of words to be guessed is indicated by holding up the appropriate number of fingers. Then the place of the word in the answer is shown by holding up the corresponding number of fingers — for instance, to indicate the fifth word hold up five fingers.

A small word is indicated by holding the thumb and first finger a short distance apart. For a big word the actor stretches out his or her arms.

Syllables of words are indicated by holding the appropriate number of fingers against the forearm; e.g. to indicate the third syllable of a three-syllable word, hold three fingers against the forearm.

The person miming the charade can let the other players know what the answer, or part of it sounds like by cupping one hand behind the ear or pulling the ear lobe, then acting out a word with a rhyming sound.

When the guessers are getting near the answer the actor makes circular movements with the hand.

To show success, the actor puts one hand on his or her nose and points with the other hand at the player who said the right word.

Who flies?

Age 6–12
No of players 6 or more

In this game players must listen carefully.

The leader can make three types of calls relating to either a bird, an animal and an elephant. All are said to be able to fly. For instance in the case of a bird, he or she might call, "Owls fly." In the case of an animal, it might be "Dogs fly." The last call is "Elephants fly."

When a bird name is called the players must flap their arms like wings. When an animal name is called players must stand still. If they make a mistake and flap their wings for a call like "Pigs fly" they are out. When "Elephants fly" is called players must run away shouting, "They would if they could but they can't," while the leader tries to catch them.

The rules of contrary

Age 6–20
No of players 4 or more
Equipment a large cloth — a scarf, a towel or even a sheet for a very large group

All players hold on to the edge of a large cloth and walk around in a circle, reciting this poem:

"Here we go round the rules of contrary,
Hopping about like a little canary,
When I say, 'Hold tight,' let go,
When I say, 'Let go,' hold tight."

The leader then promptly says, "Let go" or "Hold tight" and anyone who makes a mistake is out.

Spin the plate

Age 7–12
No of players 5 or more
Equipment a tin or plastic plate

For this game the players form a circle with one person in the middle who has a tin or plastic plate. The middle player spins the plate, at the same time calling out the name of another player, but looking at someone else. As soon as the named player realises he or she has been called, they must try to catch the plate before it falls over. If they are successful they become the next spinner. If not they are out of the game.

Shunting

Age 7–12
No of players 4–40
Equipment whistle

An outdoor game, or a vigorous game to be played indoors in a large room or hall.

All players line up at one end of a playing area or hall, except "It" who stands in the centre with a whistle. On the sound of the whistle everyone must start running towards the other end, and reverse direction when "It" blows the whistle again. The game finishes when someone manages to get to the other end, or when everyone is exhausted.

Table soccer

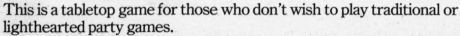

Age 6–adult
Time 5 minutes minimum (games *can* last for hours)
No of players 2 or 4 (2 pairs)
Equipment table
  cloth or blanket
  cardboard boxes for goals
  3 tiddlywinks counters
  4–10 "men" per player (Smurfs, Lego or cardboard figures, beans, coins, etc.)
  ruler (to decide centre line and for measuring distances between counters)

This is a tabletop game for those who don't wish to play traditional or lighthearted party games.

First, cover a table with a cloth or blanket. Then place a cardboard box "goal" at each end of the table, with open ends towards the centre as shown. Players or teams should have an equal number of "men" — four–10, depending on the size of the table. Each player or team has a tiddlywink counter to play with, and a tiddlywink counter is also the "ball". Before starting the game the players lay out their "men" on the table (limit the number allowed within 45 cm of the goal boxes to two at each end).

Play begins at the centre line, after a toss to decide who shall lead off. The "men" themselves cannot move, but the tiddlywinks "ball" is moved by the player whose "man" is nearest the ball. Each player aims to shoot the tiddlywink down the table to the goal, moving it from one of his or her "men" to another. A missing aim that takes the tiddlywink closer to one of the opposition's "men" changes the direction of play.

After a goal is scored, the ball is put in at the centre line by someone from the team that did not score.

Statues

Age 6–10
No of players 4 or more

This is a game to test how quickly players can "freeze" into "statues" when the call is made.

One player is chosen to be "It", and the other players dance and move about. When they have been moving for a few minutes, "It" turns his or her back and whirls around, then calls out, "Statues!" The moving players must freeze immediately in whatever positions they are in at that moment. The last to stop moving at each call is out.

Toss the feather

Age 6–20
No of players 4 or more
Equipment a sheet or blanket
            a feather or feather-shaped piece of paper

Place a feather or the piece of paper in the middle of a sheet or blanket and have everyone hold onto the edge of the material. On "Go" all players shake their piece of blanket as hard as they can. If the feather falls off, the players on each side of where it falls get a minus point. The person with the score nearest to zero after three minutes is the winner.

Queenie

Age 6–12
No of players 4 or more
Equipment a ball

In this game one player is "It" or "Queenie".

Queenie stands facing away from the other players and throws the ball over one shoulder. One of the players catches it and holds it behind his or her back, and the other players also hold their hands behind their backs. When they are ready they call, "Queenie," and Queenie turns around and tries to guess who has the ball. If he or she guesses right the game continues as before. If the guess is wrong the person with the ball becomes the new Queenie.

Easter bonnets

Age 7–adult
Time 10 minutes
No of players any
Equipment complete newspapers
rolls of Sellotape
or pins

In this game the party-goers make beautiful or amazing bonnets or hats from newspaper. Each player has their own complete newspaper and a roll of tape or a set number of pins (say, four). They must stop when the time is up.

The winner is the player who has made the best hat, by common vote. Have a parade of Easter bonnets at the end of the game.

Missing person

Age 7–12
No of players 6 minimum

Sit the players in a circle and let them select one to be "It" to start the game. "It" then walks around the outside of the circle, approaches a player and taps him or her on the shoulder, saying, "Have you seen my lost child?" The player replies, "What do they look like?" and "It" begins to describe someone else in the circle. As soon as either the person being described or the player who asked the second question realises the identity of the lost child, the two jump up and race around the outside of the circle and back to their own seats. "It" takes the seat of the slower player and that person becomes the next "It".

Scissors, paper, stone

Age 7–12 (also for teenagers as a group game)
No of players pairs or teams

The idea behind this game is that stone can make scissors blunt, scissors can cut paper, and paper can wrap up stone.

The signal for stone is a clenched fist, the signal for paper is a hand held out flat, and the signal for scissors is two fingers extended in a scissor-shape.

Teams or individual players challenge each other by simultaneously indicating one of these categories by gesture.

The game is started with the players calling out one, two, three, then quickly holding out one of the signals. If both give the same signal the game is a draw. The winner of each round scores one point.

When playing as a team, the team members must first huddle together to decide a first, second and third strategy (in case the other team produces the same signal). To score as a team the winning group each time must chase the losing group and anyone they catch must join their team for the next round. One team wins when they have captured all the opposition players.

Another category for team play is the signal "dynamite", when all the team members leap into the air shouting "dynamite", then chase the opposition regardless of their signal. This choice should be limited to once per team per game.

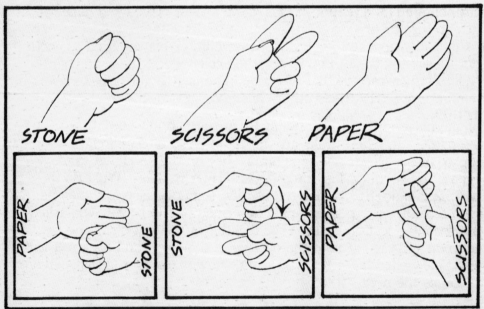

STONE   SCISSORS   PAPER

PAPER / STONE   STONE / SCISSORS   PAPER / SCISSORS

Cat's cradle

Age 7–20
No of players 6 or more

All players except one hold hands and form a circle. (If there is a very large group of players, divide into two smaller groups with only one group forming themselves into a circle). The single player(s) stands with his back to the other players. Those in the circle then duck under and over each other's arms, still holding hands, until they form a complicated tangle. The player who stands apart, or the second group, turns around and then attempts to untangle the others by instructing them to move whichever way seems most likely to untangle them. The tangled players must not release their hand holds.

Hit the deck

Age 7–15
No of players 4 or more

A vigorous party game with a nautical flavour, which has the "sailors" scrambling in all directions. This game is best played in a bare hall with no furniture.

First, identify the four walls of the room or playing area as north, south, east and west. The leader then calls one of these and all "sailors" must race in that direction. The last to get places in each round are out. Try these other calls, too.

"Hit the deck" — all players fall flat.

"Man overboard" — players may rush to any wall.

"Captain's coming" — players stand at attention and salute.

"Climb the rigging" — players move into any position in which their feet are off the floor.

"Man the lifeboats" — players sit down with their legs in the air and make rowing movements with their arms.

Pass the stick

Age 7–12
No of players 4 or more
Equipment a stick or long bottle
radio or record player

All players sit in a circle, with one person holding a stick or bottle. Music is started and immediately the object is passed from player to player. As soon as the music stops the player holding the object must put it to a pretended use and the other players must guess what it is. Some examples: a violin bow, a rolling pin, or an ostrich's neck.

Alternative: play with a ball and pretend it is another round object.

Predicament

Age 8–20
No of players 3 or more

One player leaves the room while the others choose a predicament (for example, a mouse up your trouser leg). The player then returns to the room and tries to find out the predicament by asking the other players what they would do if it happened to them.

Chinese whispers

Age 7–20
No of players 10 or more

All players form a circle or line for this game. The first player thinks of a message to be whispered down the line. The best messages for this game are complicated and nonsensical, full of similar sounds. The first player whispers the message once to the second, and so on. When the message has gone right around, the last player must tell what he or she heard, and the first player reveals what was sent. Here's an example: "I'm sure I saw something sinister standing stock-still six stairs up."

Send a picture

Age 6–20
No of players 4 or more
Equipment pencils and paper

This is a pictorial version of the above game. All players need their own pencil and paper.

The first player must draw a reasonably detailed picture (like the one illustrated) and show it to the second player for the slow count of three. The second player then draws what he or she has seen, shows it to the third player, for three seconds, and so on. At the end of the game, compare the first picture with that drawn by the last player.

A second picture may be sent off by another player after the first has passed two or three players.

Winking

Age 8–20
No of players 6 or more
Equipment playing cards

Seat all the players in a circle and deal a card to each player. Be sure the jack of spades is one of the cards dealt.

In this game the jack of spades represents the murderer, so whoever has that card is the murderer. The murder weapon is a wink.

Tell everyone to look at their card secretly. Players must try to guess the identity of the murderer before the murderer catches their eye and winks at them. As players "die" they quietly fold their arms without giving away who "killed" them. If a player challenges someone who is not the murderer, they are out.

Send a face

Age 8–12
No of players 4 or more

This game works on the same principle as Whispers and Send a picture, but this time the line or circle of players must move behind a screen or door when it is their turn.

The first player pulls a face at the second, the second player repeats it for the third and so on. When the final player receives the face he or she shows what was received and player one shows what was sent. Body antics can be used, too.

John Brown's body

Age 8–20 (family groups)
No of players 4 or more
Equipment various items prepared to feel like parts of a body

This game is played in the dark, and quite a lot of preparation must be done beforehand — in fact, the body of the deceased John Brown must be reassembled for the game.

Players sit around a table and pass pieces of the "body". They must guess what the items actually are. The leader adds the spice to the game with a gruesome commentary:

"Here is John Brown's eye," the leader says, passing a peeled grape.
"This is his tongue" (a slice of moist meat).
"Here's his brain" (a greased cabbage head).
"And his teeth" (nuts).
"His veins" (cooked spaghetti).
"His big toe" (a carrot).
"His windpipe" (a greased hose).
"His hand" (a glove filled with damp sand and tied at the end).
"His ear" (a dried apricot), and so on.

Equipment large tablecloth
a selection of items with different textures

You can also play this game without the help of a body, as a "pass and guess the object" game. To play it in semi-darkness, have a large cloth over the table and don't allow peeping. (My worst experience in this game was feeling a soft-shelled young snail that was passed around for guessing!)

Up Jenkins

Age mainly 8–20
No of players a large group
Equipment a table big enough to seat all players
a 1p piece

In this game players try to pass a coin from one to the other with their hands beneath the tabletop, without being spotted. One player is chosen to be "It". Their role is to try to pick out who is holding the coin.

The players are given the coin and are allowed five seconds to start passing it around. Then "It" can make one of these two calls:

"Up Jenkins!" The players hold their hands up in the air, concealing the coin if they have it.

"Smashums!" The players crash their hands flat on the table, concealing the coin if they have it.

After either of these calls "It" calls "Down Jenkins," and the players lower their hands and continue passing the coin. At least five seconds must pass between calls.

When "It" spots the coin, the player trying to conceal the money becomes the new "It".

If there is a number of older players in the group (say 11+) some quite young players could also be included and helped along.

Variation 1: There are three other calls that can be allowed, to make the game harder.

"Crawlers!" The players place their fists quietly on the table and slowly open out each finger till their hands are flat, but concealing the coin.

"Open windows!" Hands are placed flat on the table with fingers apart, but hiding the coin.

"Lobster pots!" Only the fingertips are placed on the table, so the hand forms a pot shape. The coin is kept hidden.

Variation 2: This game can be played by two teams: one team has the coin, and the other forms a group of watchers, who consult each other and agree on the next call they will make.

All change

Age 8–15
No of players 8 or more

All players form a circle, sitting or standing and spread out to at least arms' length. "It" is in the centre. Each player in the ring is given a number, starting at one.

"It" calls out numbers, at least two at a time, and the numbered players must immediately change places. If "It" can grab a place before one of the players, that person becomes the new "It". After a couple of rounds people become confused about where they must dash to, which adds to the fun of the game.

The merry-go-round can be made more exciting by calling out "all odds" or "all numbers below six".

Musical sets

Age 8–15
No of players a large group
Equipment radio or record player

This is a variation of musical chairs. When the music stops in this game players rush to form groups of a previously announced number. This is usually a number which will leave a player "out" in each round. (For example, for 13 players the first number could be three or four, the second number could be five, and the third number could be three again. In the second and third rounds two players would be out in each round.)

Similarities

Age 8–adult
No of players 2 or more
Equipment magazine
scissors
light card ⎱ (optional)
paste ⎰

Before the party make a large number of picture cards using magazine pictures. They should be as different from each other as possible. Either just cut them out or cut and paste them onto light card.

Players take turns to pick up two cards each and find a similarity between them and announce this to the other players. They must try not to miss turns, but find something similar between two of the remaining cards each time.

Towns and cities

Age 8–adult
No of players 6 or more
Equipment selected magazine photographs

The preparation for this game takes some time, but it is fun if you have a good supply of magazines, a free evening and a friend to work with.

The object of the game is to guess the names of towns and cities from magazine photographs of things that represent or even sound like the names of the towns chosen. For instance, Cardigan is an easy one. Bridgwater could be indicated with one or two pictures, depending on whether your bridge picture also showed water, and Braintree could have the first picture showing a "brainy" person, the second containing a tree. Try also Ringwood, Bankshill and Wrestlingworth (each two pictures).

If possible, try to use the name of familiar villages, towns or cities in your own area.

The price is right

Age 8–adult
No of players 4 or more
Equipment newspapers or magazines
scissors
prepared advertisements

Cut out a selection of advertisements of items for sale and separate the prices and keep them secret. Players must guess the advertised prices. Give three points for the best guess, two for second and one point for third.

For a variation of this game, cut off the product names and let players guess what the advertisements were promoting.

Famous faces

Age 10–adult
No of players 4 or more
Equipment pictures of people from magazines and newspapers
paste
paper
pins

Save pictures of well-known people, paste them on sheets of paper and pin them up for a who's who guessing game. If a face is very well-known, use only part of it. Just the hair, eyes or mouth is enough to identify some personalities — for instance, Charlie Chaplin's moustache. Leave the game pinned up during the party so players can think about it between other games.

Advertisement jumble

Age 10–adult
No of players 4 or more
Equipment newspaper
        paper
        paste
        scissors

Make a note of the contents of several newspaper advertisements and cut up the actual advertisements into various pieces (separate pictures, prices and captions, or even separate the words). Players must reassemble the ads as best they can.

What letter?

Age 9–15
No of players any

The players sit in a circle, ready to answer questions asked by the leader. The leader has a five-question routine. Each answer must begin with the same letter, which is chosen by the first player. The leader calls on people to answer in a random order. Players must provide an answer before the count of five (10 for small children).

Here's how it goes:

Leader: "Name the letter. 1, 2, 3, 4 . . . ."
Player: "A"
Leader: "Name the ship. 1, 2 . . . ."
Player: "Alice" (It must be a female's name.)
Leader: "Name the captain 1, 2, 3, 4, 5 . . . ."
Player: "Andrew."
Leader: "Name the cargo 1, 2, 3 . . . ."
Player: "Apples."
Leader: "Name the destination 1, 2, 3 . . . ."
Player: "Athens."
Phew! That player made it.

Newspaper headings

Age 10–adult
No of players 4 or more
Equipment a prepared selection of headlines from old newspapers
        paste
        paper
        pins

Plan well ahead for this game, or have a good supply of old newspapers.
Hunt for 10–20 ambiguous headings, paste them on sheets of paper and pin them up. Players must try to identify the topic they headed. (Save the articles to match them with later.) Leave this game pinned up as well.

Make an ad

Age 10–adult
No of players 4 or more
Equipment newspapers
        scissors
        prepared example of an amusing ad

In this game, each player or team uses words cut from a newspaper to concoct an amusing advertisement. Before starting the game, show the players an example that has already been prepared. Let the children judge the winner themselves.

Doodles

Age 10–adult in some settings
No of players 4 or more
Equipment pencils and paper

A simple game in which each player does a doodle or drawing, then passes it on for the next player to add to. If there are more than four players, have several doodles in progress and declare each one finished after it has been worked on four times.

53

What am I like?

Age 11–adult
No of players several individuals, or groups of 4
Equipment pencils and paper

In this game, sensitivity to a person's character is the key factor.

Each player or group writes the names of the other players down the left-hand side of a piece of paper. Then the page is divided into columns with the categories listed at the top. These could be things like "colour", "flower", "car make", "pudding", "type of chair", etc.

The players then try to describe each other with an item from each category, and write them in the appropriate columns. For example, what type of flower or colour does the person call to mind?

Remember, sensitivity is important in this game. Use only reasonably complimentary analogies!

Snip, snap

Age 10–20
No of players any

This is a race for answers. The leader calls out any three-letter word and points to a player. The player must call back any three words beginning with the letters in the original word before the leader can count to 12.
Leader: "Cat. 1, 2, . . ."
Player: "Crumbs."
Leader: "3, 4, 5, 6, . . ."
Player: "Angelic."
Leader: "7, 8, 9, . . ."
Player: "Toffee."
Great, got there.

Murder

Age several players over 12 years
two or three 8–10-year-olds can be included
No of players 8 minimum
Equipment pack of cards
a completely darkened house

This game requires a number of stout-hearted players and a completely darkened room or house. It must be played at night, even without firelight. If you have a fire burning cover the fireguard.

From a pack of cards take one for each player. Make sure the ace of spades (detective) and the ace of diamonds (murderer) are included. Shuffle the cards and hand them out so the players can see only their own card. Whoever has the ace of spades is the detective and must stand by the light switch. The lights are turned off and the other players move about the house. The person with the ace of diamonds (the murderer) selects a victim, and pinches him or her. The victim must give a spine-chilling scream and fall to the ground. The detective must count to three, turn on the lights, then rush to the scene of the crime. Between the scream and when the lights are turned on only the murderer may move. All players then assemble around the "corpse" and the detective must try to discover "who dunnit". Everyone but the murderer must tell the truth about their movements and experiences in the dark when the detective questions them. Have as many rounds as your nerves can stand!

If the detective is a very young player, include an adult to help out.

Sardines

Age 7–20, or family groups
No of players 4–20
Equipment plenty of hiding places (a bare hall will not do)

This is a very cosy hiding game. One player sets off to hide while the others count to 100 together. Everyone then sets off to find the first player. When he or she is discovered by one player after another the other players must squash in and hide there too, until there is no-one left looking.

The person who found the hiding place first is the hider in the next round.

Change seats

Age 8–15
No of players 4 or more

This is a useful game to play if you have no music for musical chairs.

All players, except one who is the "caller", sit in a circle. The caller cries out, "Change seats, change seats," (any number of times) and then either, "The king's coming," or "The king's not coming." If the king is coming everyone must change seats, but not with a neighbour. If the king isn't coming, no-one must move; any players who jump up are out.

Either have one caller for the whole game or let the caller dive for a seat at the appropriate time. Whoever is left without a seat then becomes the new caller.

Traditional party games

Many people know the following traditional party games. Use this list as a reminder if you need a few more ideas for younger players.
Ring a ring o' roses
Hide and seek
Musical parcel
Musical chairs
Oranges and lemons
Here we go round the mulberry bush
Here we go gathering nuts in May
Donkey's tail
What's the time, Mr Wolf?
Simon says
I sent a letter to my love
Farmer in the dell
Hokey cokey
Noughts and crosses with teams

Scavenger hunts

There are several ways of organising a scavenger hunt. Either make a list of items or answers to be found and send off a copy with each player or team so they can be ticked off as they're found, or have the players or teams bring back items or answers one at a time and then ask for the next item on the list.

All these scavenger hunts take five minutes or longer. The length of each game is determined by the length of your list. All these games require some preparation, and the more you put into it the more interesting the game will be.

Any number can play, but four is a good number for the Alphabet hunt.

Standard scavenger hunt

Age 6–adult, depending on items chosen
Equipment various items found near playing area
prepared list

This hunt involves ordinary items found anywhere. Try things like these: a round stone
a feather
a dog hair
an ice-lolly stick
a bus ticket
a can tab

Alphabet hunt

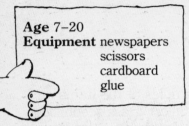

Age 7–20
Equipment newspapers
               scissors
               cardboard
               glue

The object of this game is for players or teams to be the fastest to
cut out of a newspaper a complete alphabet and glue it in order on a
piece of card.

For a more difficult version of the game, allow only capital or
lower case letters, or ask for both for each letter.

Quality scavenge

Age 6–adult, depending on items chosen
Equipment prepared list of various items to be found near playing area

In this game players must look for the *best* examples of the items on the list — for instance the longest leaf or the tallest grass seedhead. Only one item from each category wins a point for the player or team.

Word the list carefully. I asked for the longest piece of wood and received a 10-metre plank that had been stored under the hall. The other players were ready to dismantle the building to match that challenge.

This idea can be used for car or bicycle rallies where the items to be found are some distance apart.

A to Z scavenger hunt

Age 7–adult
Equipment various items found near playing area

Working indoors or out, players or pairs of players look for items beginning with each different letter of the alphabet. For example.

A: an apple tree leaf, or an animal, or an aphid (or even an appetite!)
B: a buttercup, bark or a brussels sprout.
C: a clover leaf, or a cat.

Ask for an item beginning with each of the 26 letters of the alphabet if there is time. Otherwise reduce the list to 20 or so, cutting out the more difficult letters like q, y and z.

Alternative: Ask players to find 12 items, each beginning with a different letter of the alphabet.

Information scavenge

Age 7–adult
Equipment prepared list
          telephone directory
          maps
          atlas
          encyclopedias

This game involves scavenging for answers in reference books, from maps, or by checking nearby places. Here are some possibilities.

How many steps are there in the staircase of your own house or a nearby building?
What is the reference library number for children's games books?
What year was Shakespeare born?
What is the distance between London and Aberdeen?
Who was England's first prime minister?
What is my telephone number? (or the dentist's, etc.).
How many houses with odd numbers are there in the street?

Include a mixture of questions requiring physical and mental activity.

Treasure hunt variation

Age 7–adult, depending on setting
Equipment prepared set of clues hidden in playing area
          prize for the end of the game (perhaps sweets wrapped in gold
          paper)

A treasure hunt is like a scavenger hunt, but the things that must be found are specially hidden. Usually there is a series of clues. For a very simple game these tell exactly where to hunt for the next clue. With some ingenuity you can devise a really tricky game in which the clues are not straightforward but must be worked out. For example, a clue might read "West side of the Sahara", meaning look under the western corner of the yellow carpet. Rhymes are better still as clues if doggerel verse comes easily to you.

It can be helpful to have the same number of clues as players, and label each clue with the name of the person who will read out the clue. This way players won't be left out or left behind.

Consequence games

These are a special type of pencil and paper game for small groups. In all these games the first player draws or writes something on the paper, then folds it over so only the edges of their marks or the last word or, in some cases, nothing, can be seen. It is then passed on to the next player, who adds to the picture or writing without knowing what went before. Some very funny jumbled pictures and stories are the result.

Consequence games usually last for five to 15 minutes. The only equipment required is pencils and paper, unless stated otherwise before each game.

Written consequences

Age 8–15
No of players 4 or more

Each player is given a pencil and piece of paper and begins by writing at the top of the page a girl's name, preceded by an adjective. The paper is folded so the writing cannot be seen and is then passed to the player on the left. Each player then writes a boy's name with an adjective, folds the paper again and passes it on. Then the players write (one thing per turn) what she was wearing; what he was wearing; what she said, what he said; what they did; and, in consequence, what everyone said about it.

Drawn consequences

Age 5–12
No of players 2 or more

Each player is given a strip of paper folded into three sections. The players first draw a head in the top section of the paper, with the lines of the neck extending slightly into the second section below. The paper is folded, then passed to the next player, who draws a trunk, extending the body lines across the fold into the third section. The paper is then folded and passed to the next player for the addition of legs and feet.

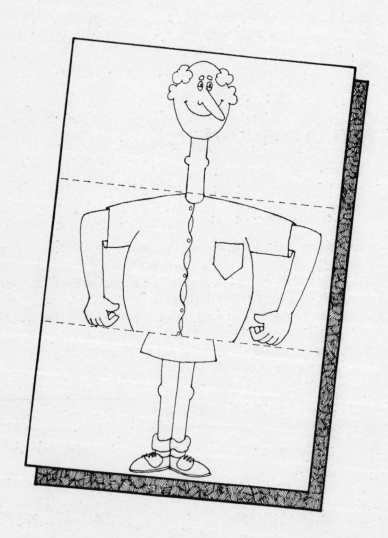

Consequence poetry

Age 9–adult
No of players 4 or more
Equipment prepared topics or metre (rhythm) to be used for the poetry

Consequence poems have an established metre and sometimes a given topic. Each player adds two lines to each poem passed to them and turns over the top of the paper, hiding all but the last word of the second line. The next player must make the first line of their contribution rhyme with the last word of the previous contribution. They should end with a new sound in the last word of the second line, and leave this uncovered for the next player to see. For example, the last words on four lines of a consequence poem might look like this:

. . . grey

. . . hay

. . . mat

. . . cat

The lines show the divisions between turns.

Consequence stories

Age 9–adult
No of players 4 or more
Equipment prepared themes written at the foot of several pages of paper

Each player is given a piece of paper with a theme written at the bottom of it. The players each write four lines of the story, and fold the paper so the entire last line is visible to the next player. The person who begins each story should also finish it, so decide the number of lines required to make a complete story and pass the papers back to the starting point at the appropriate round. (If this is not done, and you are playing with a large group — say 25 people — the game would result in some rather long tales!) Five or six contributors is about right.

Consequence book reviews

Age 12–adult
No of players about 9
Equipment a prepared page for each player (see below)

For this game pages can be prepared beforehand, listing the information required from each player and leaving several lines of free space for the answers. Each player adds their contribution, then folds the paper so their answer is entirely hidden from the next player, and passes it on.

These are the headings:

Title
Subtitle
Author's name (real or imaginary — answer with a name that has a double meaning, if you can think of one)
Brief extract — prose or poetry (limit number of lines)
A second extract
Extract from review
Name of publication reviewing the book
Another review
Name of publication reviewing the book.

If you don't have nine players (one to answer each question) cut down the number of questions asked.

Wills

Age 12–adult
No of players 4 or more

For this game of consequences there are given questions which the players must answer in turn, without seeing any of the previous players' contributions. They are:

1. The name of the will-maker.
2. The name of the beneficiary.
3. What is being bequeathed?
4. Why are they being given this bequest?
5. What conditions apply?
6. What is the reaction of the beneficiary?

Laughing games

Laughing games are good for breaking the ice near the beginning of a party or group session. They're also good for occupying a small group at short notice.

All these games can be played for about five minutes. For most of them no equipment is needed and minimal preparation time is required.

Copycat

Age 6–12
No of players 4 or more

Seat all the players in a circle. The first player starts the game by slowly and solemnly doing something to player 2 (for instance pulling a face, pressing his or her nose). Player 2 then does it to player 3, and so on. As soon as anyone speaks or laughs they are out.

Player 2 starts the second round and decides on the next action to be sent around the group.

Ha, ha, ha

Age 7–12
No of players 4 or more

This game is played in turns around a circle of players. Player 1 starts the game by saying, "Ha." Player 2 says, "Ha, ha," player 3 says, "Ha, ha, ha," and so on. Each successive player adds on one more "ha". Anyone who actually laughs, smiles, grins or "has" out of place is out.

Poor pussy

For this game the players sit in a circle and choose one player to take
the first turn at being "pussy". The player chosen must crawl around
the ring of players, who take turns to stroke "puss" and say "Poor
pussy" three times. If anyone laughs or smiles while they are
stroking "puss" they must take puss's place.

Fish and chips

Age 7–12
No of players 3 or more

One player is chosen to be "It". Everyone else takes turns to ask him or her questions and, with a perfectly straight face, "It" must answer, "Fish and chips."

The game might go like this:

"What's your name?"
"Fish and chips."
"What do you want for your birthday?"
"Fish and chips."
"What is your hairstyle like?"
"Fish and chips," and so on.

"It" counts up the number of questions he or she is asked before laughing and going out.

Antics

Age 8–adult
No of players 6 or more
Equipment none absolutely necessary, but some may help. Strange clothes could be used.

Divide the players into two teams and give the first team one minute (or 45 seconds) in which to make the other team members laugh. Any players in team 2 who laugh must drop out, and team 1 is awarded a point for each success.

Then team 2 has a turn to make the members of team 1 laugh.

Laughing ball

Age 8–12
No of players 6 or more
Equipment a ball

In this game one person is chosen as thrower and the others stand in a semi-circle. The thrower tosses the ball towards the players, who toss it back as soon as it is caught.

They must laugh when the ball is out of the thrower's hands and stop laughing when he or she is holding it. When they make a mistake, players drop out or exchange places with the thrower.

Laughing square

Age 8–12
No of players 6 or more
Equipment a square of cardboard, white on one side and black on the other

This is similar to the game above. Players form two teams — the blacks and the whites. This time a square of cardboard is thrown instead of a ball, and one person acts as a thrower to both teams.

When the white side of the card lands up, the whites must laugh until the card is picked up for the next throw. When the black side faces up, it is the blacks' turn to laugh. The penalty for mistakes is to join the other team.

Throw a smile

Age 8–15
No of players 6 or more

Everyone sits in a circle, looking very solemnly at each other, and one person is chosen to begin. The player chosen gives a big grin, wipes their hand across their mouth and "throws" the grin to someone else, who promptly sends it on the same way. Anyone who laughs or grins at the wrong time is out.

Talking games and crazy conversations

In these games players must be careful not to say the wrong thing. Each game lasts about five minutes. Check below for the best number of players, age groups and any equipment needed.

I love, I hate

Age 4–6–adults in some settings
No of players a large group or individuals in circulating pairs

This is a conversation game in which players tell each other their main loves and hates in chosen subject areas.

Choose wide-ranging topics like puddings, colours, films and car makes. Avoid subjects where the players' feelings may be hurt — for example, people, or political parties.

Sausages and chips

Age 6–12
No of players 4 or more

Choose a simple, *familiar* story and read it to the players once, telling them to listen carefully. Then explain that the next time it is read they must say "sausages" every time you come to a word starting with "s", and every time you come to a word starting with "c" they must say "chips".

Here is an example. "Sausages" and "chips" are said instead of the words bracketed:

"Once upon a time there was a little girl chips (called) Goldilocks. Sausage (she) lived with her mother in the woods. One sausage (spring) morning sausage (she) sausage (said), 'I will go for a walk.' "

Yes, no beans

Age 8–adult
No of players 4 or more
Equipment a supply of beans, buttons or 1p pieces for each player

First, each player is issued with an equal number of beans (or buttons or coins). The object of the game is for players to talk among themselves, trying to persuade the others to say "yes" or "no".

For every "yes" or "no" a player persuades another to say, he or she is paid a bean. But if that player says "yes" or "no", he or she must pay a bean to whomever they are speaking to.

To make the game more difficult, add "sometimes" and "never" to the list of taboo words.

This is Boxer

Age 7–20
No of players 6 or more

This is a good game for introducing people.

All players sit in a circle and the first three — we'll call them Simon, Stephen and Janet — begin. The first player must have something to hold to represent Boxer the dog.

Simon turns to Stephen, holding the "dog", and says, "My name is Simon and this is Boxer." Stephen then asks, "Does he bark?" Simon replies, "He barks."

Stephen then says to Janet, "My name is Stephen and Simon says this is Boxer." Janet then asks, "Does he bark?" Stephen then turns back to Simon and repeats the question, "Does he bark?" Simon replies, "He barks," and Stephen repeats this to Janet: "He barks."

And so the dialogue proceeds around the circle with each player checking back about whether Boxer barks. Each succeeding player will have to repeat the names of all the previous players, until finally it is the last player's turn. The last player will have to recite everyone's christian names and that Simon says this is Boxer. The game ends with Simon saying, "I know, and he barks." By this time everyone will be quite sure of all the other players' names.

Fizz-buzz

Age 8–15
No of players 4 or more

There are three variations of this game: Fizz, Buzz and Fizz-buzz.

It is a talking game in which the players sit in a circle and count, with each player saying one number. However in the game of Fizz, the number five is taboo, and the player must say "Fizz" instead. Any multiple of five is also said as "Fizz".

In the game of Buzz, seven is taboo, and so are any numbers containing seven and multiples of seven. The word "buzz" must replace all of them.

Fizz-buzz is even harder. In this game both five and seven and their multiples are taboo.

Choose the game to suit the age of the players.

La-di-dah

Age 8–20 (family groups)
No of players at least 5
Equipment an object for each player — for example, a pencil case or an apple. Try not to use very small items

This is another game of co-ordination, this time with a satisfying, dance-like rhythm and chant.

This is the chant:

> "La-di-dah
> La-di-dah
> La-di-dah-di-dah-di-dah."

Players form a circle, each with an object placed in front and slightly to their right.

On each "la" the players pick up the object. On the last "dah" of each line of the chant they move their object across to their left. This means that on the last line they move the object as follows, holding on to it until the final "dah":

> La-di-dah-di-dah-di-dah
> Right to left to right to left (let go here)

Gradually speed up the game and keep playing until the rhythm becomes hilariously muddled.

Salespeople

Age 8–adult
No of players 6 or more
Equipment a supply of buttons or beans for the members of one of the teams

For this game the players are divided into two teams, customers and salespeople. Each customer is given 10 beans or buttons and the salespeople select a product they'd like to sell — anything from ice-cream to corn plasters. The object of the game is for the salespeople to earn beans by persuading the customers to say "yes", "no" or the name of the product. They are allowed two minutes, after which the customers must add up the number of beans they have left.

The beans are then given to the other team, who become customers, and the new salespeople have a chance to revenge themselves on the other team.

How many beans?

Age 8–20
No of players 4 or more
Equipment 10 beans for each player

This game is tricky to explain, so have a practice first to make sure all players understand how to do it.

Each player hides a few beans in one hand, then moves among the other players challenging them to guess how many he or she holds. If a player guesses too high, he or she must give the challenger enough beans to make up the number. If the guess is too low, the challenger must give the guesser the number of beans guessed. If the guess is right, the challenger must give the correct number of beans to the guesser.

In each contact with another player each person must have one turn as challenger and one turn as guesser.

Players drop out when they run out of beans. Either let the winner be the person with the most beans after five minutes, or continue until one player has all the beans.

Here is the dog

Age 8–20
No of players 6 or more

In this game two or more messages are passed around a circle of players at the same time.

Start with player 1 saying, "Here is the dog."

Then player 2: "The what?"
Player 1: "The dog."
Player 2: "Here is the dog."
Player 3: "The what?" and so on.

The message is passed right round the circle with all players repeating this dialogue in turn.

From the other end of the circle, send off the message: "Here is the cat" in the same way. If the group is large, send off other messages about animals at intervals. The fun comes when the messages "pass" each other around the circle.

Pippity pop

Age 8–15
No of players 6 or more

This game is played with a circle of fast talkers — an uneven number of players works most easily.

The first player says "pippity pop", the next, "poppity pip" and so on, alternating until a mistake is made. Anyone who gets it wrong must drop out, and the game continues.

This is my nose

Age 8–20
No of players 5 or more

For this game players sit in a circle and one person is chosen to begin. Player 1 says to player 2, "This is my nose," but points to his or her knee. Player 2 says to player 3, "This is my knee," while pointing to his or her nose. The two statements are passed around the circle until someone makes a mistake by pointing to the right part of his or her body. Anyone who makes a mistake is out.

If the group is small or has an even number of players, reverse the statements at the beginning of the second round or add a third statement — for example, "This is my knee," while pointing to the shoulder; then, "This is my shoulder," while pointing to the nose; then, "This is my nose," while pointing to the knee.

Whiz bang

Age 8–20
No of players 6 or more

In this game players form a circle and call out either "whiz" or "bang". If "whiz" is called, the person on the left of the player who made the call must respond. If "bang" is called, the direction of the game changes so that the player on the right responds next with "whiz" or "bang". "Whiz" responses go around the circle in whatever direction they started from until someone says "bang".

Start the game with the first player calling out "whiz". This game can be quite exciting, with whizzes and bangs flying back and forth around the circle.

Talking contest

Age 8–adults in some settings
No of players 2 groups (large or small), and a referee

The aim of this game is to say as many words as possible and to keep talking for as long as possible.

Team members take turns to talk. They can say whatever they like — sentences or unconnected words — but not the same word over and over again. As soon as the first player stops or slows down, the second team member takes over, and so on. If any player does not run out of words he or she must stop after one minute and let the next player take over. The referee keeps the time.

If the groups are large, have more than one referee and let the teams play at the same time and compare times at the end.

Railway carriages

Age 10–adults
No of players groups of 2
Equipment prepared topics

In this talking game one player tries to lead the conversation in certain directions. When the other player guesses the subject, he or she tries to steer the conversation away from it.

In each group, one player (A) leaves the room and player B is given three statements which he or she must work naturally into a conversation with A within five minutes.

As soon as the topics are given out, player A returns and both players talk. A tries to prevent B making any of the three statements without, of course, knowing what they are. The game ends when B makes the third statement or after five minutes of effort.

75

Rhythm

Age 7–20
No of players 4 or more

This is a rhythmic game of co-ordination between actions and speech.

First, all players form a circle and are numbered consecutively (1, 2, 3, 4 and so on). They then work up a rhythm of two hand claps onto their knees, followed by two ordinary hand claps, one click of the fingers of the right hand, then one click of the fingers of the left hand. This is easier to work out if the players say in unison, "Slap, slap, clap, clap, click, click" as they do it. When the rhythm is established one player is chosen to lead. That player (say no. 1) calls out his or her number while clicking the fingers of their right hand, then the number of another player (say no. 3) while clicking the fingers of their left hand. Player 3 must call "three" when everyone next clicks their right fingers then another number (not one) when everyone clicks their left fingers. Carry on the routine, gradually speeding up the rhythm until the players make mistakes.

Although in the above example player no. 3 cannot call "one" (the number of the previous player) he or she may call any other number that has already been called.

For a faster version of this game allow only one clap on both knees and hands before making the finger clicks.

Penny games
(or 5 or 10p games if you're rich!)

Here are some games with a currency exchange to add spice to your party or games session. A couple of pounds' worth of 1p pieces from the bank will go a long way.

Alternatively, use buttons or beans. Any other equipment needed is listed below.

The first three games are suitable for individual players seven to 12 years. For Heads and tails divide the players into pairs. Five to 10 minutes is a good time to expect the games to last.

Hide and seek

Equipment 1p pieces to hide
Sellotape or Blu-tack

This game involves quite a lot of preparation, but the more time spent organising the game the better.

Hide in separate places a number of 1p pieces where they will be visible without the players needing to move anything. Use Sellotape or Blu-tack to stick them in unlikely places. Keep a note of how many are hidden so you will know when they have all been found. Each player keeps the coins they find.

Penny roll

Equipment cardboard for prepared target grid
1p pieces

Make a target grid on cardboard as shown and "seed" it with various
coins — 1p to 20p in whatever arrangement you fancy. Give each
player a supply of 1p pieces to roll onto the grid from a distance of
about three metres. If their coin lands clearly inside a square, they
scoop the contents. If it falls on a line, the coin is moved into the
nearest square and remains there as part of the target loot.

The penny drops

Equipment 1p pieces
milk bottle
chair

The object of this game is to drop 1p pieces into a milk bottle placed
on the ground. Players must drop them from the height of the back
of a chair, with their wrists steadied on the chair back. Begin by
handing out five or 10 coins to each player and let them play in turns.
Players are allowed to keep every penny they get in the bottle.

Blindfold games

This section contains a varied selection of blindfold games for players six years and upwards. Check before each game for suggested ages, but remember the success rate in each game must be high enough to keep everyone enthusiastic. Try the targets and distances before starting the party or games session.

Allow about five minutes for each of these games. Suggested numbers of players and extra items of equipment needed are listed below.

For blindfolds, use large brown-paper grocery bags placed over the heads of the players. *Do not use plastic.*

Thief, thief

Age 6–12
No of players about 6
Equipment blindfold
newspaper
various goodies such as shoes, a rubber, pencil, plastic cup,
matchbox, cotton reel

One player is chosen to be a blindfolded shopkeeper, who must sit behind a tray of wares armed with a rolled-up newspaper swatter. The other players sneak up from their bases on the other side of the room and try to pinch the goodies one at a time. If the shopkeeper hits a thief (and he or she should do their best) the thief must return to base empty-handed before making another attempt on the loot. Remember, only one thing at a time may be stolen.

The winner is the most successful thief.

Bell-ringer

Age 6–12
No of players 6 or more
Equipment blindfolds
              bell (optional)

For this game, all players except one are blindfolded. The sighted player either has a bell to ring or decides on a noise to make. The blindfolded players must try to catch the bell-ringer by following the sound of the bell or the calls he or she makes. When a player catches the bell-ringer they become the new bell-ringer.

Hunt the slipper

Age 6–15
No of players 6 or more
Equipment blindfolds
              shoes belonging to players

Before putting on their blindfolds, all players take off their shoes and pile them up in the centre of the room. Then, with the blindfolds on, they hold hands and walk in a circle around the pile three times. On "Go" all players race to the pile and try to put on their own shoes. This game can also be played in the dark without blindfolds.

Cat and dog

Age 6–12
No of players 2 or more
Equipment blindfolds
              table

This is a chasing game for two blindfolded players, one pretending to be the cat, the other the dog. The game is played around a large table, and the cat and dog start off on opposite sides, each keeping one hand on the table. On "Go" the dog sets out in pursuit of the cat.

Horatio

Age 7-15
No of players 6 or more
Equipment blindfold
          chalk
          newspaper

For this game, mark two chalk lines down the floor to represent a bridge. One player is then chosen to be Horatio and is blindfolded and guided to the centre of the "bridge" where he or she sits down. Horatio is armed with a newspaper whacker.

The other players must try to sneak past Horatio without being hit. Any player who is whacked is out. Those who succeed in getting past must hop quietly back across the bridge, again without being hit.

If you have a big group and enough space, give Horatio "two more to help me" as the original Horatio had.

Horatio

Then out spoke brave Horatius,
The Captain of the Gate:
"To every man upon this earth
Death cometh soon or late.
And how can man die better
Than in facing fearful odds
For the ashes of his fathers
And the temples of his Gods,

Hew down the bridge, Sir Consul,
With all the speed ye may;
I, with two more to help me,
will hold the foe in play.
In your strait path a thousand
May well be stopped by three:
Now who will stand on either hand
And keep the bridge with me?"

Lord Macaulay

Top hat

Age 7-20
No of players 3 or more
Equipment pencils and paper
          blindfolds
          prepared list of subjects

Give each blindfolded player a piece of paper and pencil and a subject to draw. (It could be a monkey or a fish, whatever you fancy.) The subject should be made as complete as possible — for instance, the monkey could be drawn with a face and a baby clinging to it.

When the players think they have definitely finished drawing, add as an afterthought, "Oh yes, give him a hat."

The winning picture is the one voted best by all the players.

Maze stunt

Age 8–20
No of players 4 or more
Equipment prepared obstacle course (see below)
blindfolds

Lay out an obstacle course across a room and let the players see what they will have to cross. Include cotton reels, trip wires, beakers full of water and even a couple of eggs. Then ask for a volunteer to lead off and try to hop the course blindfolded with the aid of the other players calling out hints. (Perhaps the offer of a small prize would encourage players to volunteer.)

While the volunteer is being blindfolded, have an accomplice replace the beakers full of water with empty ones and the whole eggs with empty shells.

Balloon games

You will need six or more players for these balloon games. Allow at least five minutes for each game, and up to 15 minutes for Balloon in the air.

Before starting these games you might like to try an air-release distance race. For this game let the players blow up their own balloons.

Balloon in the air

Age 6–15
Equipment a balloon

All players form a circle and each player is given a number. The balloon is tossed into the centre of the circle and, when the leader calls their numbers, the players must give the balloon another pat into the air. Players drop out if the balloon falls to the ground when it was their responsibility to pat it up.

If playing with a large group, renumber the players when the leader can no longer remember which numbers remain to be called out.

Balloon pass

Age 8–15
Equipment a lightly inflated balloon for each team

The members of each team form a row, then race to pass their balloon along the line using only their chins and chests. Any player who drops their team's balloon must pick it up and take it back to the first player, and the team must start again.

Hop and pop

Age 8–20

Equipment a balloon and cotton string for each player *or* a paper balloon shape for each player

This is a game of simultaneous defence and attack. All players have a balloon (or paper balloon shape) tied to one of their ankles with cotton. Players must try to defend their own balloons while trying to pop the other players' balloons. As soon as a player's balloon is popped, he or she is out.

Alternative: play the game in pairs, with each player challenging his or her partner. The winner of each round then challenges another player, and so on.

Relays and team games

For relays and team games the leader or organiser should be well-prepared, with a whistle, a watch with a second hand and pencil and paper or blackboard and chalk ready for scorekeeping. The instructions for the games should be as clear and as brief as possible. Plan the sequence of games before you start. Ten to twenty minutes' worth of varied games, mixed with games from other sections, make a satisfying session. Make up a timetable of vigorous games or running relays mixed with quiet games, but be ready with more in case one game is unpopular or the programme moves faster than expected. Avoid repeating a popular game on the same day. It is better to keep enthusiasm high — a second round may not be as successful as the first. On the other hand, all the games are fairly brief. If the group is obviously enjoying a certain game, don't cut it short. Make sure, too, that the children do not spend so long watching each other compete that they get bored.

Relays work best with small groups where everyone can remember everyone else and turns come round quickly. We found that four is an ideal number per team, and three to seven is quite good. Where a special number or different number of players is required this is noted above each of the games.

If there is an uneven number of players, have some team members "run" twice, or rotate two players in some teams. The player who stands down may be a helper for that round, keeping the score or holding a stopwatch.

With large groups, run trials and send each team champion in to the next round. While the winners are playing in the semi-finals and finals, run corresponding semi-finals and finals for the losers' teams.

All these games are suitable for players six or seven years or older unless otherwise stated. If there is a wide age range of players present make sure the teams are made up of fairly equal numbers of older and younger players.

Simple equipment is needed for most of the relays and team games in this section. Make sure it is ready beforehand.

Tournaments are the answer if equipment is limited. They are also good for occupying small teams for set periods of time. Each group moves from one activity to the next, adding to their score as they go. Make sure each game in the tournament occupies a similar amount of time.

See the sections on quizzes for more games that can be played with small teams.

Clothing count

> **Equipment** plenty of clothing, jewellery and other accessories

In this game team members swap visible clothing among themselves, and the other team must guess which items have been swapped. Start the game by lining up two teams opposite each other and allow the players half a minute to look closely at what the members of the other team are wearing. Teams then move out of sight to change visible clothing, swap hair clips and jewellery and change hairstyles. Allow three minutes. Ask each team to choose a scribe to record their findings. Set a time limit of two to three minutes for the recording.

Potato peeling

> **No of players** this game can be played by individuals or teams
> **Equipment** potatoes
>   kitchen knives

The object of the game is to make the longest piece of peel not thicker than 3 mm. Players with thicker peel are disqualified. If the teams are large, provide several knives and potatoes per team and let each player peel until his or her piece breaks. Award points for the longest piece of peel and for the first potato completely peeled. (Note: peeled potatoes may be kept white by immersing them in a pot of water with a little milk added.)

Paper strip

Equipment paper of any size and type, but the same for each team or person
scissors for each team

This is played in the same manner as the above game, but with paper and scissors instead of potatoes and knives. Players try to make the longest continuous paper strip from one sheet of paper. Give a time limit if this game is part of a games session with lots of other activities planned. With no time limit this activity may last half an hour, or even longer — and give great satisfaction.

Carrot rings

Equipment carrots
kitchen knives

While you have the knives out for the potato-peeling game, why not try a carrot-cutting race as well? Provide several carrots per team and allow each player to cut carrot rings as fast as they can for half a minute, counting the rings at the same time and adding their total onto the team's score.

String winding

Equipment 12-metre balls of string

Ask the team members to spread out an arm's length away from each other. Give a 12-metre ball of string to the first person in each team. The object of the game is a race to unwind the ball of string as it is passed to each player. It must not be dropped. Award points to the fastest team, then make them race to wind up the string as it is passed from player to player. Again, the fastest team wins.

Add up

Equipment pencil and paper for each team
ruler
tape measure

In this game each team adds up the following:

— the shoe sizes of all team members (specify that all members should count the same kind of footwear, either shoes, gumboots or sandals).
— the heights, widths of finger spans and/or waist measurements of all team members.
— the number of brothers and sisters each team member has.
— the number of people who live in each house occupied by a team member.
— the birthday dates (day of month) and telephone numbers of each team member.
— the number of pets belonging to each team member.
— the months of each team member's birthday (that is, count 1 for January, 2 for February and so on).

The winning team is the team with the highest score.
Vary or lengthen the game by adding your own ideas.

Send-a-message race

Equipment pencils and paper
throat tablets for the players
ear plugs for the organiser!

Divide each team in half into senders and receivers. Ask the senders to stand at one end of a long room or, if outside, to stand at a set distance apart. Each group of senders is allowed one minute to make up a 10-word message, which is then shouted in unison to the receivers, who must try to understand the message. Messages to all receivers are sent at the same time, from the same end of the room. The winning team is the first group to understand the message. In the next round the senders become receivers.

This game may be simplified by the organiser preparing a batch of 10-word messages in advance.

Ma and Pa race

Equipment an equal number of items of clothing for each team — e.g. apron, belt, tie

For this race the members of each team split into pairs. At the starting point, player 1 is handed the apron and player 2 the belt (or tie) which they must put on each other simultaneously. When ready, both players run arm in arm to a preset goal and back, untie the other's belt or apron or whatever and hand them to the next pair of players.

Grandpa's slippers

Equipment large pair of slippers or shoes for each team
dressing-up clothes (optional)

Find a pair of slippers or shoes for each team. The bigger they are the better. Each player must put them on in turn and race to a preset goal. This game can be made even more interesting by providing other dressing-up gear which must also be worn in the race.

Candle douse

Equipment 1 candle per team
1 tin per team
squeeze bottles filled with water
paper tissues

Stand a candle in a tin for each team and provide squeeze bottles full of water. Each player must light the candle, *walk back* 2 metres and douse it with a squirt of water, then hand the bottle and matches to the next player. Everyone but the first player must gently dry the wick with a paper tissue before relighting the candle. After each team member has had a turn, hand out mopping up gear!

Candle lighting

Age 6–(appeals to teenagers)
Equipment candle and a box of matches for each team
Highest score seen by author 72

In this game players light a candle as many times as they can with one match. Once a wick is hot it is possible to light it and blow it out very quickly.

This game can be played individually (works well for teenagers) or in teams with each player adding to the team's score. Play the game through twice.

Equipment 2 candles
             2 tins
             2 boxes of matches

Place two candles in two separate tins halfway up the room — one for each team. The task of each player is to run up and light the candle, blow out the match, run to the end of the room and touch the wall, then run back to the tin, blow out the candle and run on to tag the next player.

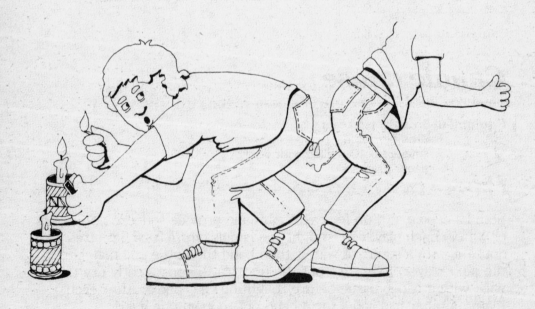

Fumble pass

Equipment a selection of objects to be passed
Choose objects of contrasting size and weight
We had a full glass of water, a potato on a spoon, a lit candle and a brick for each team
Other ideas: a saucer of marbles, a playing card with an eraser balanced on it

For this game the members of each team form a row. Team members must pass a selection of objects from the first player to the last along the row as quickly as possible. As soon as the object is received by the last player, he or she calls out "Now," and the first player picks up the next object. To make the game more difficult, pass two objects at a time, one from each end of the row.

Variation 1: With the team in a line, pass objects overhead from the front to the back of the line.

Variation 2: Try passing cups using the little finger of the right hand only.

Variation 3: Pass a mixture of objects behind the back.

Matchbox lids

Equipment matchbox lids

Arrange players in rows, as for the previous game, and pass matchbox lids from one player's nose to the next.

Pass the Polo

Equipment half a drinking straw or a toothpick for each player
Polos

Arrange the players in rows and provide each player with half a straw or a toothpick, which is held in the mouth. The players pass a Polo along the row from straw to straw without touching the Polo.

91

Straws and paper

Equipment a piece of a drinking straw for each player
10cm square of paper for each team

In this game players line up side by side in teams and pass a square of paper from one player to the next by sucking it up with their straws. If the paper is dropped the person who was passing it must suck it up from the floor.

Alphabet chain

Equipment pencils and paper

Each player has half a minute in which to write down as many letters of the alphabet as possible, starting at A, then from where the previous player left off. The winning team is the one that has the most written when time is up.

Nursery rhymes

Equipment dice

The object of this game is for each team to sing until they can remember no more nursery rhymes, or until one team pauses longer than it takes the other team to count to 10. Toss a dice to work out the order in which each team has a turn and give an extra point to each succeeding team (that is, one point to team 2, two points to team 3 and so on) because their tasks are progressively harder. (They must not duplicate rhymes already sung.)

Slide a coin

Equipment a coin for each team
a piece of card for each team member

Provide a card for each team member and a coin for each team. The players hold the cards in their mouths and slide the coin along their row from card to card.

Move it

Equipment 2 containers for each team
sand, water, wheat, confetti or flour
spoons

Place a container at each end of the room for each team. Leave one empty and fill the other with sand, water, wheat, confetti or flour. Team members must scurry up and down the room, transferring spoonfuls of the contents of the full container to the empty container. Let each player have turns until time is up, or specify two turns each and see which team finishes first. There could be extra points to the team that makes the least amount of mess. Have cleaning gear handy.

Fan race

Equipment 1 piece of paper per team
1 plastic plate or equivalent per team

The members of each team take turns in a relay race to fan a piece of paper down the room with a plastic plate or icecream carton lid.

Beans race

Equipment 2 bowls per team
dried beans
1 drinking straw per player

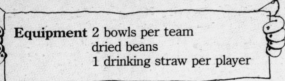

Provide each team with an empty bowl at one end of the room and a small bowl full of dried beans at the other. Give each player a straw. Let the team members take turns to suck up beans with their straw and race to the other end of the room, then deposit the beans in the second bowl. The next player starts as soon as the previous player's load drops into the bowl.

Alternative: have small teams — pairs or threes — and let all the team members play at the same time.

Buttons

Equipment buttons
fabric
threaded needles

Set a time limit of three minutes and start a button-sewing race. Specify that each button must be sewn tightly with no fewer than three loops of thread.

Necklace

Equipment nylon fishing line
beads, buttons or drinking straws cut into equal small pieces

This is a threading race. Each player must thread four items, then pass on the necklace to his or her neighbour. The team that finishes first is the winner.

Streamers

Equipment at least 2 pairs of scissors
newspaper cut in strips 6 cm wide

This is a cutting race. If you have enough pairs of scissors everyone can be in the race at the same time. If not, hold elimination rounds, with one person from each team competing in heats and the winners going on to the semi-finals and finals.

The object of the game is to cut down the lengths of newspaper, forming two strips. For the semi-finals, ask the winners of the previous races to take one of the narrow strips they have made and race to cut them in half again. Provide the finalists with even thinner strips to show their style. If the strips are broken during the race the player is out.

Mobius strip

Equipment at least 2 pairs of scissors
strips of paper or newspaper
glue or adhesive tape

Another cutting race, and this time the results are rather
unexpected. There are two ways of making mobius strips:

1. Take a strip of paper and twist once before joining both ends.
   Next cut down the middle of the strip, while keeping the ends
   joined. The strip will fall into a long, continuous band.

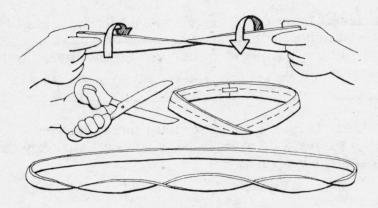

2. Twist the strip *twice* before joining the ends. Cut down the middle
   of the strip, as shown. This will form two interlocking rings.

   According to how many pairs of scissors you have, divide the
   teams as described for the previous game and start a Mobius-strip-
   cutting race.

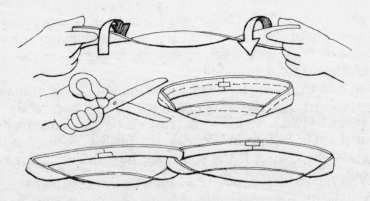

Paper clips

Equipment a supply of paper clips

Distribute an equal number of paper clips to each team. All players may participate at once, making the paper clips into a chain as quickly as possible.

Whooooo

This is a contest to make the longest sound (all players must make the same whooing sound). Each team should hold its own heats and send forward their best player to compete against players from the other teams in a final.

Length?

Equipment pencils and paper (long strips)

Give each team a pencil and suitably sized piece of paper. Each player must try to draw a line 3 centimetres long, starting at the point where the previous player left off. When every player has had a turn, measure the lines and award points to the team closest to the correct measurement. Try with other lengths, too.

Time?

Equipment a watch with a second hand, or a digital watch

In this game each team member guesses when half a minute has passed. The second player starts as soon as the first player says "now" to indicate the time is up. If there are four players in each team, the team that finishes nearest to two minutes is the winner.

Size?

Equipment pencils and paper

Each team member must draw the shape of an object as near to the correct size as possible. Make sure the objects are not in sight. Some examples: a matchbox, various coins, a milk bottle.

Cards

Equipment a pack of cards for each team

Give out well-shuffled packs of cards and have the teams race to lay out the suits in numerical order.

Bean sort

Equipment 500g bags of mixed beans or other known volumes of beans
tray or tabletop

This game is a race to sort out different varieties of beans from a 500 gram bag, or other known amount, of mixed dried beans. Provide each team with a tray or tabletop to use as a working surface.

Needle and thread

Equipment needles
spools of thread (as many as possible)

Set a time limit of three minutes and have a needle-threading race between the teams.

Blindfold relays

The simplest way of blindfolding players quickly is putting a large brown-paper grocery bag over the head. *Do not use plastic bags.* Here are some games to try blindfolded.

Sorting

Equipment blindfolds
a bowl for each team containing three types of assorted items (beans, buttons, paper clips, matchsticks, bottle tops)
3 saucers for each team

The first player in each team is blindfolded and handed a bowl containing the mixture of items and three saucers to sort them into. As soon as the task is completed the first player tips the items back into the bowl and passes them on to the next player, who is then blindfolded.

Walk the plank

Equipment long wooden plank or planks
furniture or other obstacles for obstacle course
bean bags (optional)
dressing–up clothes (optional)

Lay out the planks on the floor and let the blindfolded players take turns to "walk the plank". If they put a foot on the floor they must begin again.

As an alternative, arrange an obstacle course for each team. The "sighted" players must instruct their "blind" team mate, then try their own luck. To vary the game, have the players race the obstacle course with bean bags on their heads or dress up at some points.

Peg the washing

Equipment length of string
pegs
washing

String the line across the room and have the blindfolded players take turns to race at pegging and unpegging washing. Players 1 and 3 can peg while players 2 and 4 unpeg.

Feed the baby

Age 8+
Equipment blindfolds
food (ice cream and cereal are good)

For this game you will need blindfolds that leave the mouth free. Use scarves, old nappies or tea towels.

The players in each team take turns at being mum or dad (player 1) or baby (player 2). On the whistle, mum or dad (who is blindfolded) races to stuff the food into baby's mouth (also blindfolded). Players 3 and 4 tell him or her where the open mouth is. When the portion is eaten, player 2 becomes mum or dad and feeds player 3, player 3 then feeds player 4, and so on. Don't make the helpings too big!

How far?

Equipment various items (see below)
tape measure

This game is a competition in throwing. Ask each team to send forward their best shot. The winner will win for his or her team.

Try throwing a variety of objects: a balloon, a balloon with a rubber tied to the string, a playing card, a straw, a handkerchief with a knot in it. Measure the distance the items are thrown.

Missile contests

Equipment missiles and targets (see below)

The success rate in this game must be high enough to keep the players enthusiastic, so try out targets and distances before starting the games. Have each team add up their own score as the contest progresses.

Here are some suggestions for missiles and targets:

Three darts to be thrown at a dartboard.

Three draughts to be rolled onto a draughts board (score one for each draught which lands cleanly within a square).

Four preserving jar rings to be tossed onto the legs of an upturned chair.

Ping-pong balls to be bounced off the wall and into an egg carton.

Bean bags or balls to be tossed into a bucket.

Marbles to be rolled into a chalked area.

A peg to be held by the teeth and dropped into a milk bottle.

A coin to be dropped into a glass submerged in a bucket of water.

Frisbee

Equipment paper plates, cut-out cardboard discs or paper darts

Use the missiles in this game as frisbees (hold horizontal to the floor and toss sideways). The game may be either a distance contest or a contest of skill. If the latter, have the players toss their missiles through a coat-hanger.

Waistband

Equipment 1 60-cm piece of elastic tied in a circle for each team

This is a relay race in which each team member must wriggle through the elastic circle, then pass it on to the next player. The first team to finish wins.

Race and carry

Equipment various items to carry (see below)

Another relay race, but this time the players must carry objects without dropping them. Some examples: a bean bag on the head, a ball or balloon between the knees, a potato on a spoon, a lit candle, some feathers or pieces of light paper on a plate, a rubber or hexagonal pencil balanced on a knife.

Tiddlywinks

Equipment tiddlywinks or corks

This is a race between teams to get their tiddlywinks or corks from one end of a room to the other.

If using tiddlywinks, give each player three turns at flipping them, then let the next player take over. If using corks, player 2 takes over where the cork lands after being thumb-flipped by player 1.

Bowling alley

Equipment plastic bottles filled with sand or water
or potatoes balanced three high
tennis balls
or small bags filled with beans, sand or sawdust

For this game make your own bowling alley with the equipment suggested above. Add up individual players' scores to get the total for each team.

Speed to a goal

Equipment broom handles, sacks (both optional)

This is a relay race in which the next team member sets off as soon as the first player reaches the goal.

Each player must think of a different method of travel — for instance, running, skipping, galloping, hopping, running backwards on all fours, bear-walking, bunny-hopping, crab-walking sideways, caterpillaring (place hands on the floor and walk toes up to fingers, then walk fingers out in front again), broomstick riding, waddling (holding the ankles), granny stepping (heel to toe), sack racing or leap frogging.

Have a players' conference first and let the children decide how they will get to the goal line.

Messages

Equipment prepared messages

For this game each team must provide a message-giver, who stands at the far end of the room ready to tell prepared messages to each member of their team.

The first player in each team runs up for their message, races back to tell it to player no. 2, who runs back and tells it to the message giver. (If the message is not repeated correctly the player must go back to hear it again.) Player 2 then takes back a new message to tell to player 3, and so on.

Team ball

Equipment ball or bean bag
             goal for each team

Arrange a goal (such as a chair) for each team and start a race to hop and kick a ball or bean bag around the goal and back. Each group should play as a team, helping each other to keep the ball moving around the goal.

As an alternative to make the game harder, have the team members bunny-hop or hop while holding their ankles.

A variation is a game in which team members take it strictly in turns to kick the ball.

Run and recite

This is a relay race in which each player runs around a goal, back to the team and, on returning, counts down from 10 or 20 or recites the alphabet backwards.

Raisin race

Equipment 1 bowl per team
raisins
toothpicks

Provide each team with a bowl of raisins and each player with a toothpick. Ask each team to form a row. The object of this race is to pass the bowl along the row as quickly as possible. Each player must feed the neighbouring player two raisins with the toothpick before passing on the bowl.

The Bicycle Petit Prix

Age works well with teenagers
Equipment one or more bicycles
stopwatch (optional)
obstacles (optional)

If you have enough bicycles, have the teams compete at the same time. Otherwise use a stopwatch to time each player. Set up a goal and have each player ride to it as slowly as possible without putting a foot down. To make the game harder, arrange obstacles along the route to the goal (as in a slalom ski run). Any player who has to touch the ground is out and the next team member must start immediately. The slowest team wins.

Legs ladder

For this game the team members sit on the floor, spaced out and with their legs apart. On "go" player 1 gets up, runs behind the team to the other end of the row, then runs over all the outstretched legs and back to his or her place. Player 2 must run over 1's legs, down the back of the team and over the rest of the legs to his or her place, and so on.

Two-at-a-time relays

> **Equipment** pre-tied, 30 cm elastic leg joiners (optional)
> ball (optional)

Players race around a goal and back, side-by-side in pairs, with their arms linked. First players 1 and 2, then 2 and 3, then 3 and 4, and so on.

Alternatives: try back-to-back with the person who led going backwards on the way back; or wheelbarrow racing, leap-frogging, three-legged racing or just hurrying and kicking a ball between partners.

Stepping stones

> **Equipment** two 20 x 20-cm squares of card for each team

In this race player 1 places the squares of cardboard on which player 2 must step to get to the goal. Player 1 moves the cards in turn while player 2 steps from one to the next. The players' roles are reversed on the way back from the goal.

Alternative: The players move their own stepping stones, one at a time, while still standing on the other card.

Specify no skidding for the first round, then have a round in which skidding is allowed.

Railroad race

The first player in each team (the engine) chuffs to the goal, back to his or her team to pick up the first carriage (next player), then back to the goal again, and so on, until the whole team forms a train and has "been there and back". One team should pant "chuff-chuff", another "choo-choo" and another "puff-puff". When the train gets in, the members of each team should whistle signal together.

Hammering race

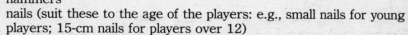

Age 8–20
Equipment blocks of wood
hammers
nails (suit these to the age of the players: e.g., small nails for young players; 15-cm nails for players over 12)

Each team is given a block of wood and a nail for each team member. Players hammer in their nails in turn, with each player starting as soon as the previous player has finished hammering. The winning team is the first to have all the nails hammered flat.

Newspaper unscramble

Age 8–15
Equipment one or more scrambled newspapers of the same length (preferably fat) for each team

This is a race to reassemble the pages of one or more newspapers in their correct order. Divide the pages between team members.

Knots

Age 8–15
Equipment 2 metres of string per team

Each team is given a length of string, in which each player must tie two (or more as specified) knots before passing it on. Start the game with a whistle. The fastest team wins.

Matchstick skyscraper

Age 8–15
Equipment a box of matches for each group
ruler

Which team can make the tallest skyscraper from matches, or which can use the largest number of matches before the skyscraper falls down?

For this game, empty a box of matches on the floor or on a table in front of each group. Players then take turns to add a match to the skyscraper. Use the ruler to decide which matchstick building is the tallest.

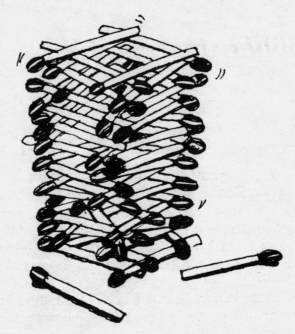

Straw towers

Equipment packet of straws
paper clips
masking tape or Sellotape

This is a variation of the above game, in which players see who can make the highest tower in a set length of time — say 10 minutes.

Two hands

Age 8–20
Equipment various items (see below)

In this game two hands are used to perform various tasks, but they must not both belong to the same player! Use player 1's right hand and player 2's left hand, then 2's right hand and 3's left hand, and so on.

Tasks to try: putting on a sticking plaster, undoing two toffees, wrapping up a parcel, peeling an orange, tying a shoelace.

Peashooter

Age 8–12
Equipment jars
     bamboo
     drinking straws (or catapults)
     dried peas
     rice

This is a game of target practice. Set up the jar (or jars) lying on its side as a target for the pea — or rice — shooter. Make the pea-shooter from a piece of bamboo and the rice-shooter from lengths of straw. Tell the players to put the rice in the shooter at the end nearest their mouths.

Remember to explain what other uses of shooters and catapults are acceptable or unacceptable, and that swallowing too many pieces of uncooked rice is bad for you.

Guess and count

Age 8–15
Equipment telephone directory
pencils and paper

In this game each player tries to guess the number of times a name is listed in the telephone book.

Give each player a different name. For instance, how many Norths, Souths, Easts and Wests are there? Other good names to try are the Matthews, Marks, Lukes and Johns, and the names of colours — Black, White and so on. Decide which spelling is to be used, in case there are variations, and let the players look up the results for themselves. Give a point for every wrong guess. For instance, if 10 Norths are guessed, but there are only six in the book, award four points. If the number guessed is four, add two points. The team with the lowest score wins. In larger cities some research beforehand might be necessary so that less common, easily countable names are chosen.

Directory race

Equipment 1 telephone directory for each team (ask several players
beforehand to bring the telephone book from their homes)
prepared lists of questions

Supply each team with a telephone directory and hand out identical lists of questions to each team before the game starts. For this game the players must race to find entries in the telephone book and call them out or make a list of answers, the winning team being the first with a completed list. For instance, what is the tenth name in the second column on page 123? and so on. Keep a list of the answers to refer to and award points for every correct answer, or say the winning team is the first to finish.

Slap-happy

Age 8–12
Equipment 10p pieces (an equal number for each team)

A relay race in which the players' hands do all the work!

The teams line up, and on "go" the first player in each team picks up a coin, places it on the flat palm of his or her hand, then slap-passes it onto the flat, outstretched hand of the next player, and so on. The coins must be passed one at a time, right along the row and back again. The winning team is the first to get every coin there and back.

All together

Age 8–12

A race in which all members of each team compete at the same time. The players link arms sideways then race while simultaneously running, hopping, jumping or shuffling without lifting their feet.

Some alternatives:

The players make a line with their hands on the hips of the player in front.

The players hold hands, but with each player's right arm threaded through their legs.

The players all sit on the ground, holding on to the waist of the player in front, and snake-sway forward to the goal.

Sit down, stand up

Age 8–20

A race in which the members of each team link arms sideways, then sit down and stand up together five times. Arms must not be unlinked. The first team finished wins.

Vigorous games

For these games you will need a reasonable amount of space. With small groups a room cleared of obstacles will do. A community hall is ideal for larger groups and, of course, they can all be played outdoors.

Check for suggested numbers of players, age groups and equipment required. Allow about five to 20 minutes for each game. Apart from a few minutes required to hide the treasure in Cats, rats, mice, there is no preparation time involved.

Nearly half of these games are chasing games, in which the size of the playing area makes quite a difference. If the area you have is very large either limit the space the players may use or have more chasers. It isn't easy to lay down guidelines about the best number of chasers as the age and energy level of the children affects the game, too; but one chaser to every four to six runners is usually about right. The chaser or chasers should have a reasonable chance of catching all the other players.

French cricket

Age 3+ (with older help)
No of players 3–12
Equipment ball and bat

In this game the batter holds the bat in front of his or her legs, and the bowler aims to hit the batter below the knee. When the batter hits the ball the nearest player tries to catch it, then has a turn at bowling. If the batter is hit on the legs below the knee, or if the ball is caught, he or she is out and the bowler of that ball becomes the new batter.

Variations: Let the players take turns at batting according to their ages, regardless of who catches or bowls a player out. If very young players are included let them have several "lives" so their turn will be of a respectable length even if they are hit or caught out straight away.

112

Broken bottles

Age 4–12
No of players 2 or more
Equipment a tennis ball, or small rubber or plastic ball (use a large ball for young players)

This is a ball-throwing game between all players.

Everyone begins by being allowed to catch with both hands. If a player drops the ball he or she may then catch with only one hand — the right hand. If they still manage to catch the ball they win back their other hand. But if the ball is dropped again, they must use only their left hand; if it is dropped yet again they must catch while kneeling on one knee; then kneeling on both knees; then sitting; then lying down. For every successful catch the player regains a position in the above sequence.

Grandma's footsteps

Age 6–12
No of players 4 or more

This game is very similar to "What's the time Mr Wolf?"

One player is chosen to be "Grandma". He or she turns away from all the other players and calls out one of the instructions given below. When "Grandma" estimates that the players are very near (but not near enough to tag her) she or he quickly turns and chases after them. If anyone is caught they become the new "Grandma".

These are the calls grandma can make:

"Umbrella steps": players must whirl around and around, moving forwards.
"Granny steps": players must step forward with the toe of the hind foot touching the heel of the front foot, and so on.
"Pin steps": players must make the tiniest steps possible.
"Shunting": players take two ordinary steps forwards then four tiny steps backwards, and so on.
"Scissors": players jump their feet together and apart continuously, moving forwards.

Dragon tag

Age 5–12
No of players 6 or more

One player is chosen to be "It" and chases the other players and tries to tag them. As the players are caught they must link arms with "It", forming a dragon chain. The outside arms of the players on each end of the "dragon" are then used to tag other players.

Variation: The dragon may split up and work in pairs whenever there is an even number of players. When a dragon of six players becomes three pairs working together they will usually manage to catch even the most fleet-footed runners.

Colour race

Age 6–12
No of players 6 or more

Players divide into two teams and stand in rows about 2 metres apart, ready to run. The leader stands in the middle.

First, each team confers in whispers and chooses a colour name for themselves. The leader then calls out colour names until one team's colour is called. They then run as fast as they can for their home line, with the other team in pursuit. Any people caught must join the opposing team. Then the players reassemble and choose new colour names.

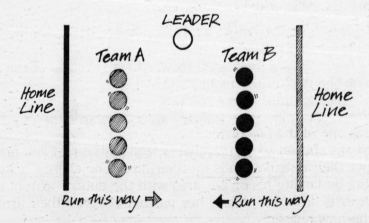

Stiff candles

Age 6–12
No of players 8 or more

If there is a small number of players one person is chosen to be the chaser. Otherwise choose several chasers.

On "go" the chasers try to tag other players, who when caught must stand straight like a candle but with their arms outstretched to the sides. Other players may free the stiff candles by touching one of their outstretched hands.

Jellyfish

Age 6–12
No of players 6 or more
Equipment a cushion

In this game players sit in a circle with linked arms around the jellyfish — a cushion placed on the floor. The object of the game is to push and pull each other into the centre (keeping arms linked) to touch the jellyfish, without getting touched by it yourself. Those who touch the cushion are out and must leave the circle, which will steadily get smaller and smaller. The winners will be a pair of players with firm feet — the only two left in the game.

Pairs

Age 6–12
No of players 10 or more

This game is one of my favourites.

One player is chosen to be the chaser, and all the rest link arms in pairs and put their outside hands on their hips. The chaser "catches" other players by linking his or her arm with the outside arm of a pair. When a player is "caught", his or her partner releases their arm and becomes the new chaser.

Battle of Hastings

Age 8–20
No of players 8 or more
Equipment a large number of tennis balls, bean bags or sneakers
a chalk line down the middle of the floor helps

First, explain that this game is to be played only by throwing at ground level. High throws disqualify a player.

Players form two teams with an equal number of missiles and line up on opposite sides of the room. On "go", the members of each team heave their ammunition at the feet of the other team. The winning team is the first to have no missiles on their side of the playing area.

Bombardment

Age 5–12
No of players 6 or more
Equipment bucket or chalk circle
bean bags or soft balls

This game is similar to Battle of Hastings, but instead there is a leader who must face up to bombardment from all the players.

The leader either has a bucket full of bean bags or stands in a chalk circle crowded with balls. The leader throws out the balls or bags as fast as possible, while the players throw them back in.

If at any time the leader can shout "Empty," he or she wins. The team wins if the leader gives in exhausted.

Cat and mouse

Age 7–12
No of players 8 minimum

All players except two form a circle holding hands with their arms outstretched. One player is chosen to be the mouse, and one the cat. The mouse begins on the inside of the circle and the cat on the outside.

The cat chases the mouse in and out and around the circle until the mouse is caught. The players who make up the circle can help or hinder the cat (whichever they please) by raising or lowering their arms.

Tishy-toshy

Age 7–adult
No of players 2 (or 2 pairs)
Equipment a tennis ball or ping pong ball
        a table (this can be any size — a coffee table or dining table)
        play in a room with few ornaments

This is a fairly vigorous indoor game in which two players bounce a ball to each other across a table.

The players stand at opposite ends of the table and take turns to throw the ball. If a small table is used, the ball must bounce once on the table. If a large table is used the ball can be bowled, rolled or bounced along the table and off the ends, but it must not go off the sides of the table. The catcher must not touch the table with any part of his or her body. If he or she touches it, or does not catch the ball, the server gains one point.

We play first to 10, then change ends. The winner is the first to get 21 points.

For another version of this game, position a 2p piece in the middle of the table. Whenever the ball also knocks off the coin, the serving player scores an extra point.

Cats, rats, mice

Age 7–12
No of players 6 or more
Equipment well-hidden treasure (see below)
a very large hall or playing area

Hide plenty of treasure (things the players would like) around the playing area. Divide the players into two or more teams of three to five members. Each team selects a leader and an animal as their team name.

When a player finds some treasure he or she stands beside it and makes the appropriate animal noise until the leader comes to collect it (only the leaders can collect the loot). Of course, a member of another team can also rush over and make their team's animal noise at the same time. The leader who arrives first picks it up.

Keep a note of the number of items hidden. When all are found and collected, let the teams settle down to divide the spoils.

This game can also be played outdoors in a large marked area.

Shoe

Age 7-12
No of players 8 or more
Equipment a bean bag or duster, shoes belonging to the players

All players take off their shoes, divide into two teams and line up on opposite sides of the room, holding their shoes. A bean bag or duster is placed in the centre on the floor. The object of the game is to move the duster or bean bag into the other team's half by throwing shoes at it. Players may use any shoes that come near them.

Surfboard

Age 7–12
No of players 6 or more
Equipment chalked circle

One player sits cross-legged in the middle of a circle of kneeling players, who must try to reach in and tag the player on the "surfboard" without being tagged themselves. When a player is tagged, he or she must change places and sit on the "surfboard".

Circular football

Age 8–12
No of players 8 or more
Equipment a large ball, cushion or a bean bag

Players form a circle, standing at arm's length apart with a leader in the centre. The leader must try to kick the ball through one of the gaps. If the ball gets through, the player on the right side of that gap becomes the new centre player.

(Wear socks or go barefoot if using a cushion as the ball.)

Soccer hop

Age 8–12
No of players 8 or more
Equipment a lightly inflated football, a bean bag or a cushion

For this game, goal areas are marked at each end of a room and the teams line up on opposite sides, ready to hop into action when the whistle is blown. During three-minute rounds players hop around and attempt to score goals without putting their other foot on the ground. If a player touches the ground a penalty is awarded to the other side.

Tug of war

Age 8–20
Equipment rope (at least 4 metres long)
chalk

Group tugs of war are really successful only with fairly small teams, four on each side seems to be the maximum number that works well.

With a rope circle

Tie the rope so it forms a circle, then get two teams inside the rope circle, facing away from each other and holding on to opposite sides of the rope. Tell them to brace themselves, then PULL!

If there are three teams, make a bigger rope circle and mark the floor with chalk to show where each team is to stand.

Tug of war without a rope

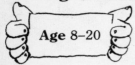

Age 8–20

For this contest ask two teams to line up facing each other. The players should hold hands alternately with members of the opposite team (that is, player 1 from team 1 holds the left hand of the first player in team 2, who holds the right hand of the second player in team 1, and so on). On the signal, both teams pull backwards as hard as they can.

As an alternative, have the players line up facing away from each other, with their arms linked alternately, as described above. On the signal the members of each team should pull *forwards* as hard as they can.

Run preliminary rounds and finals, with winners taking on winners.

Pole push

Age 8–20
Equipment a long, stout stick

Line up a team on each side of the stick or pole. The players should grip the pole, with their arms straight. On the signal, both teams shove for all they're worth.

Last pair out

Age mixed
No of players 16 minimum

Here's a chasing game for a large number of players of varied ages. Have the players line up in pairs, holding hands. Pair older players with younger ones so all the pairs have an equal chance.

To start the game, the last pair in the row drops hands and runs up their side of the row to the front of the row, with the second to last pair of players in pursuit. The second to last pair cannot tag either of the last pair until they move forwards, so they may move back or circle sideways and choose their moment to make a dash for the front. If they manage to reach the front without being caught they rejoin hands and call, "Last pair out." The chasers must then drop out. If the chasers catch the runners, they become the front pair and also call "Last pair out." As soon as this call is heard the new last pair drops hands and runs to the front with the new second to last pair in pursuit.

Piggy-back soccer

Age mixed (older players should carry younger players)
No of players 8 or more
Equipment a ball
a marked goal area at each end of the room

Players form two teams, then choose partners from their own team. Partners must piggy-back each other while attempting to score goals for their team. Time each round to suit the players' stamina. Mounts become riders in the second half if the players are mostly of the same age.

Mind reading games

Here are some puzzles which call for a special kind of insight or a quick eye. Any number can play, although make sure you have 10 or more for Trains and stations, which is not strictly the same type of game. These games are suitable for players eight years and over, unless otherwise stated. Any equipment needed is listed before the games.

In many of these games the leader has an accomplice, who is infallible. The other players must try to read the leader's mind, or work out how the accomplice knows the answers. Before each game (or, preferably, before the session or party) the leader and accomplice need to get together to work out their strategy.

This row, that row

Age 6–12
Equipment various small objects (see below)

Select a number of objects that can be laid out in two rows on the floor or table. Let your accomplice look at them, then send him or her out of the room. Ask the audience to choose one of the objects for your accomplice to guess.

When your accomplice returns, point to the objects, one by one, asking, "Is it this?" or "Is it that?" When you reach the chosen object, the audience will be astounded to see that the accomplice recognises it at once.

How did they do it? The trick is that you and your accomplice decide earlier that the top row is "this" row and the bottom row is "that" row. You can give your accomplice the vital clue by saying "Is *this* it?" when pointing to something in the bottom or *"that"* row.

Alternatively, play the game with four rows of objects, labelled alternately "this" and "that" rows.

Black magic

Age 6–15
Equipment objects in playing room (see below)

This is a variation of the above game, in which any object in the room may be chosen. The clue for your accomplice is that the chosen object will be the one you point to immediately *after* pointing to a black object.

"Who is it?"

In this game there is no accomplice, so the person who leaves the room must work out the answer for themselves.

The player who leaves is told that those who remain will pick someone as "It", and when he or she comes back into the room he or she is to work out who has been picked by questioning everyone else. Once the player has left the room the game's organiser explains that they will choose no one person to be "It" — the solution for each player being "the person on my left". The answers thus may be mystifying to the guesser at first because each person answers as if the person picked is the person on their left. (See the example in the picture.)

This game can only be played once at any party.

1. **2.**

Questioner asks Simon to describe 'It'. Simon describes Stephen who is on his left.

Questioner asks Stephen to describe 'It'. Stephen describes Janet who is on his left.

Tower Bridge

Age 6–20

For this game challenge everyone to watch what you do, then copy your action exactly.

For instance, say "Tower Bridge has an arch spanned by two drawbridges, and two towers," while drawing it in the air with your *left* hand. Anyone who uses their *right* hand has got it wrong. Be sure to let them say and draw the whole thing before telling them if they have done it wrong, especially at the beginning of the game.

Pass the scissors

Age 6–12
Equipment scissors (optional)

In this trick game a pair of scissors, real or imaginary (two fingers held out), are passed around a circle of players "crossed" or "uncrossed". To be right in this game players must say "crossed" or "uncrossed" if their knees are respectively crossed or uncrossed as the scissors are passed. The leader lets the players know whether their calls are right or wrong, and the players must work out why.

Legs

Age 6–15
Equipment objects in the playing room (see below)

For this game make the audience's mystery object the thing pointed to *after* asking the accomplice whether it is a person, chair, or television set (in other words, the thing indicated *after* pointing to any object with *legs*).

Sixty-seven

In this game the accomplice must guess a mystery number decided by the audience.

   The clue for the accomplice is given in the first answer. For instance, the leader may start by saying, "Is it 67?" The *first* numeral in the *first* question (6) tells the accomplice when the answer will be said. In this case, the answer will be contained in the *sixth* question asked.

Martian maths

Age 7–20
Equipment matchsticks

The leader and a friend begin this game by explaining that they can read Martian.

   The leader makes patterns on the floor with matchsticks and asks the accomplice to read the Martian numbers made by the patterns. The other players try to guess how the accomplice knows the correct answers.

   The accomplice will always be right, because the leader secretly indicates the required answers by holding out the correct number of fingers so the accomplice can see them.

Trains and stations

Age 6–adult
No of players 10 or more

In this game players form a circle by holding hands, and one player is chosen to stand in the centre as "train spotter". Another player from the circle is chosen as the leader, who is responsible for "putting trains on the track". Every fifth or sixth player in the circle is a "station".

When everyone is ready, the leader sends off a train by squeezing one of the hands he or she is holding. When a player feels a "train" (hand squeeze) he or she must send it on by squeezing the hand of the next player. Players who are "stations" may delay the train or reverse its direction, and must toot when it has left them.

The train spotter in the middle must attempt to find the train and, when successful, changes places with the player who gave the hand squeeze that was seen.

Car

Age 6–15
Equipment playing cards

Place three cards in a row in front of the audience and explain that your confederate, who is out of the room, will be able to tell which card they have picked as soon as he or she walks in. The audience then makes its choice, the accomplice is called in and he or she points straight to the correct card, as promised.

The secret lies in the way you call in the confederate. The code word is "CAR". "C" stands for "Come in", which means it is the first card. "A" stands for "All right", which means it is the second card, and "R" stands for "Ready", which means it is the third card.

Card code

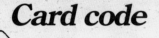

Age 12–20
Equipment playing cards

This is a more complex version of Car. It is another game in which a confederate can read the leader's mind and guess any card in the pack.

While the confederate is out of the room, the group picks a card and the leader lays it on the table. Then the confederate returns. He or she can tell, by the code, the suit of the card:

Card placed at top of table = hearts.
Card placed at right side of table = clubs.
Card placed at left side of table = spades.
Card placed at bottom of table = diamonds.

Let's say the card is the queen of hearts. It will therefore be placed at the top of the table. The confederate then asks "Red?" the leader's reply tells him or her what part of the pack it is in:

"Yes" means it is an ace, 2, 3, or 4.
"Right" means it is a 5, 6, 7, or 8.
"Good" means it is a 9, 10, jack or queen.
"Correct" means it is a king.

In this case the leader's answer will be, "Good."
The confederate then states the name of the suit: "Hearts?"
He or she will then be able to tell the exact card by comparing the leader's next answer with the previous answer.

"Yes" means it is a 3, 6 or 9.
"Right" means it is an ace, 5 or 10.
"Good" means it is a 2, 7 or a jack.
"Correct" means it is a 4, 8 or queen.

In this case the answer will be, "Correct." The accomplice already knows the rank of the card is not a 4 or an 8 from the previous answer, so he or she can triumphantly announce, "Queen of hearts."
The code is quite a lot for the leader and confederate to remember, but this is an impressive trick to watch.

What's the catch?

These games are often good for filling lulls in a games session or a party — for instance, when the party is beginning and some of the guests haven't arrived, when food is being brought to the table and when guests are leaving.

No equipment is needed. The games can be played by children eight years and older and take about five minutes each. Any number can play.

All these games have a similar form. All players except one or two are "Its" and they must all guess "the catch". Alternatively, one player is chosen to be "It". That player must leave the room while "the catch" is explained to the other players. Don't leave it too long before telling "It" the answer if they can't guess, otherwise the game will be too frustrating.

Shopkeeper

All players except the "Its" repeat in turn, "My father is a shopkeeper and he sells . . . ." The name of the goods must be something the speaker is touching with his or her body.

The "Its" have a chance to join in as soon as they have guessed the catch.

Grandmother's tea

In this game the first player might say, "My grandmother likes tea but not coffee." Player 2 might say, "My grandmother likes football but not soccer." Eventually, "It" or those players who are not in the know may guess that all the things granny likes have the letter "t" in them.

Players may decide that grandfathers like the reverse, coffee but not tea. The catch now is that they like only things with double letters in them — they like the moon but not the sun, balls but not bats.

The "I know" club

This game is similar to the previous game, but players who know the catch are part of the "I know" club. In the "I know" club anything that does not contain the letter "i" is all right.

So, player 1 might say, "I know football is a good game. Athletics are no good, though." Player 2 might say, "I know Monopoly is okay, but not Master Mind."

Trips

In this game each player says they are going on a trip and taking something that starts with the initial letter of their first name. Or, to make it more difficult, something that begins with both their initials. Players take turns to speak.

*M*ichael might say, "I'm going on a trip and taking a *m*ouse."

*P*aul might say, "I'm going on a trip and taking a *p*lant."

In the more difficult game, *T*ania *S*cott might say, "I'm going on a trip and taking a *t*errible *s*pider."

When any of the "Its" think they have worked out the catch, they suggest something to take themselves.

Train trip

Begin this game by asking who is good at arithmetic. When you hear that some of the players think they have some skill, ask them to try this one.

"A train left London Bridge Station (substitute the names of local stations) with 10 people on board. At Camberwell it picked up four passengers and lost two." Pause long enough for your audience to work this out, then go on to tell how many passengers got on and off at any of the next five or six stations. The speed and difficulty of the story should be related to the age of the audience. Just when the players think they finally have the answer worked out, ask, "How many times did the train stop?"

Who's the leader?

All players except one form a circle, and the player who is to be the first guesser leaves the room. The circle chooses a leader, then the guesser is called back to guess who it is.

Before the guesser enters the room, the leader begins doing an action (say, nodding the head) which the other players copy. After the guesser has returned, the leader must try to change the action (say, opening and closing the mouth) when the guesser is not looking directly at him or her. Everyone else must copy the action. When the guesser discovers the identity of the leader, they change places and the leader becomes the next guesser.

Bang, bang

The organiser of this game explains that he or she will "shoot" someone from the group of players, but that the gun being used is very strange. The bullets do not always go where they are aimed, yet there is a pattern in the way they work. The players' task in each round is to guess who has been shot.

The organiser then "shoots" one or more people by holding out two fingers and saying, "Bang, bang!" The dead person is the first one to speak after the shooting. (It can be the organiser who was shot.)

Card games for large groups

Here are some card games involving either luck or skill, or a mixture of both, which can be played by fairly large groups. Suggested ages are given before each game.

The role of the dealer changes in a clockwise direction for each hand. In all these games play begins with the player on the dealer's left. Jokers are used only in Penny on the lady and Group gin rummy. Aces are low (that is, they count as one) in every game except Oh hell!

Pelmanism (or Pairs)

Age 3+, with older friends
No of players 2 or more
Equipment a pack of cards

This is an excellent first card game for small children. The aim of the game is to collect pairs of cards.

1. The pairs of cards are laid out face down at random on the tabletop. For a very young child playing with one other person, begin with only three or four pairs of cards and gradually build up to using the whole pack. Picture cards may be used provided there are pairs or sets of four.
2. When the cards are laid out players take turns to turn over any two cards.
3. If the cards form a pair, that player keeps them. If they don't match, the player turns them face down again in the same place as they were originally, after everyone has had a good look at them.
4. The winner is the player who gets the most cards.

In our family we began playing so that the children would win most of the time. Soon we had our work cut out to beat them!

Sevens

Age a game for anyone old enough to learn the card number sequence
No of players 8 maximum
Equipment one pack of cards

The aim of this game is to play all your cards before the other players, and to do this in such a way that the others are prevented from playing theirs. It's mainly a game of luck, although a little skill is involved.

1. Shuffle a pack of cards and deal the whole pack (some players may end up with one extra card).
2. The player who has the seven of diamonds begins play by putting this card face up on the table.
3. The next to play is the person on this player's left. They may put out the six or eight of diamonds or any other seven.
4. Play continues clockwise around the table, with everyone playing a card of a face value bordering the cards already on the table. Sevens may be played at any time.
5. Players cannot miss a turn if they hold a card that can be played.
6. If a player cannot play a card, he or she passes by knocking on the table.
7. Throughout the game players attempt to block other players' turns by carefully selecting the cards put out. A key card which a player is able to keep for some time is called a "woof" card.
8. The winner is the first player to play all the cards in their hand.

Chase the ace

Age 3+, with older friends
No of players any number; large groups can play
Equipment one pack of cards (ace low)
              chips (matchsticks or counters)

In this game each player has several chips to represent "lives". The aim of the game is to try not to lose any lives. A life is forfeited by the player with the lowest card at the end of each game. Depending on the number of players, the rounds can be quite quick.

1. The dealer shuffles the pack of cards and deals one card to each player, starting on the dealer's left.

2. If any player is dealt a king they must immediately turn it face up in front of them. The king acts as a block (see below).

3. Then, in turn, and starting at the dealer's left, the players decide whether to keep their card or exchange it. Players can swap their card only with the player on their left, who has no choice but to change cards if asked.

The decision about whether to change cards is based on the rank of the card. Because the person with the lowest card has to pay a life at the end of the game, nobody would want to keep an ace. A two would always be changed, and it is usually a good idea to swap if you have a three. But if the person on the player's left has a king they cannot swap cards and must keep the card they have. The player on the right who wants to change cards is blocked.

4. When play reaches the dealer, he or she may choose to keep the card dealt (or the card received from their neighbour), or cut the pack and take the card that turns up.

5. Now all players turn up their cards and the player with the lowest card pays a life.

Prize cards

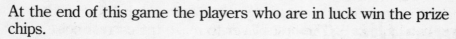

Age 5–adult
No of players any number up to 52
Equipment 2 packs of cards
         chips (counters or dead matchsticks) for betting

At the end of this game the players who are in luck win the prize chips.

1. Each player is given three chips.

2. The dealer deals four cards face down in a row from the first pack.

3. Each player puts one of their chips onto three of the four face-down cards.

4. The dealer deals the second pack of cards as equally as possible to all the players. All the cards must be dealt out.

5. The dealer now puts out on the table the remaining cards from the first pack, one at a time, face upwards. Players with matching cards (of the same number and suit) put their cards out on the table as the matching cards are turned up.

6. Eventually only four cards will remain with the players. The dealer then turns up the card with the fewest chips on it and the player with the matching card wins the chips. Then the card with the next

lowest number of chips is turned up, and so on, with the players with matching cards winning the chips.

Appoint a new dealer for the next round.

Menagerie

Age 7+, family groups
No of players 7 (play with one pack), or larger numbers (12 is ideal). Use 2 packs
Equipment 1 or 2 packs of cards

In this game individual players aim to collect a large pile of cards — the whole pack if possible. This is really a game of luck, although some skill is required in the speed of players' reactions.

1. Each player in turn chooses an animal and practises making the noise that animal makes. Go around the group to hear each one.
2. The dealer shuffles the cards and deals seven to each player (the number can be reduced for a large group playing with one pack of cards). These cards are placed face down in a pile on the table in front of each player.
3. One-by-one, and starting on the dealer's left, players turn up the top card on their pile, forming another pile of face-up cards. If someone turns up a card of the same face value as a card already turned up, they immediately make the animal noise belonging to the holder of the other card. The owner of the first card of the pair races to make the animal noise chosen by the player who has just turned up the matching card. The first player to make the correct noise wins the other player's pile of face-up cards and places them under their other cards.
4. The game continues until one player wins all the cards or most of them.

A variation of this game is known as "Shops". In this version each player owns a shop (for example, a chemist's or a drapery). As pairs of cards are turned up players race each other to give the name of an item from the partner's shop.

Pig

Age 5–12
No of players up to 13
Equipment pack of cards

In this game players try to obtain sets of four matching cards.

1. Sort out the same number of sets of four cards of corresponding face value as there are players.
2. Shuffle these cards and deal each player four, face down.
3. Each player then looks at his or her cards and, together with the other players, passes on one card to the player on the left. Some people find it a good idea to count at each pass, "One, two, three, pass."
4. As soon as a player holds four matching cards they put a finger on their nose. The players watch each other for this sign and must copy as soon as they see someone hold their finger on their nose. The last player to notice loses that round.

Penny on the lady

Age all ages. Even very young children can be helped to play
No of players 6 is ideal, especially with youngsters. With older groups large
numbers can play
Equipment chips (matches or counters)
a pack of cards (ace low) plus a joker, and 4 extra queens from
another pack

This is a kind of group patience game of luck in which the aim is to collect chips.

1. Each player is given eight matches.
2. The four extra queens are placed in the centre of the table.
3. Before play begins, players place bets in the kitty and on a "lady" (one of the queens). In our version of the game the bets are as follows:

1st round: 1 in the kitty, 1 on a lady
2nd round: 1 in the kitty, 2 on a lady
3rd round: 2 in the kitty, 2 on a lady
4th round: 2 in the kitty, 3 on a lady
5th round: 3 in the kitty, 4 on a lady

If players have only one or two matches left we allow them to try for one last round, even though they don't have the right number of matches.

4. The entire deck of cards is dealt into equal piles — one at a time for each player and one for a dummy hand. The dummy hand is sorted into suits, in order, and placed face up on one side of the table so all players can see the cards.
5. The player on the dealer's left puts out his or her lowest card. Players put out their cards in this suit, according to what is in their hands, working up in order. When the next card in a series is in the dummy hand the last player able to put down a card puts down their lowest card of any suit and starts a new run.
6. Play follows this pattern until someone is able to put out a queen from their hand. They then collect the matches on that queen.
7. The first person to play all their cards (this may be before any queens are played) collects the chips in the kitty.

Group gin rummy

Age all, except very young
No of players large groups
Equipment two packs of cards, including jokers

The objective of group gin rummy is for each player to get as low a score as possible. This game is a test of players' skill in deciding which cards to keep.

1. The dealer deals out seven cards to each player and places the pack face down in the middle of the table. The top card is turned face up and placed beside the pack.
2. Starting on the dealer's left, the first player takes either the exposed card or the top card from the pack, then discards one card (it can be the card just picked up) and places it face up beside the pack. Play continues like this clockwise around the table.
3. Players choose whether to take the exposed card, and which cards to discard, by relating them to the other cards in their hand. Each player tries to gain a hand that scores low.
4. This is how the hands are scored:
Sets do not count against the player. For example:
Three of a kind (say three jacks) counts zero.
Three cards in a run (say nine, 10 and jack) counts zero.
(Note that a card which is part of a run cannot also be used as one of three of a kind or another run.)
A flush (a hand made up of any cards all of the same suit) counts zero.
A straight flush (a run of seven cards all of the same suit) wipes out the whole score standing against the player from previous rounds.
A hand containing seven of a kind (say seven kings) also wipes out any previous score.
Jokers can be included and they can act as any card of any suit. Cards not in sets are scored on "pip" value (face value).
5. *Rumbles:* When the score in a hand adds up to 10 or less the player knocks on the table (rumble) on that player's next turn and every player must lay down their hand for scoring. The game continues until someone "rumbles".
6. When a player's score reaches 100 he or she is out of the game. The later stages of the game are usually quite fast.
7. If the centre pack is used up before a player is out, the discards are shuffled and turned face down.

Oh hell!
(or Oh deary me! — our granny's name for this game)

Age 11–adult
No of players 3–8 or 9
A useful game for teaching novices about tricks and trumps
Equipment one pack of cards (ace high)

This game is a mixture of luck and skill, in which players try to forecast the number of "tricks" or rounds in a hand they will win before play begins. The ace is the highest card in the game, and the cards belonging to the suit that is "trumps" are higher than all the other cards.

1. The dealer shuffles the cards and deals them out. In each round a different number of cards is dealt. Start with one card for each player in the first hand, and progress upwards one-by-one until the whole pack is split equally between players (for example, 13 cards for each of four players). Then progress back down to one card per player.
2. After dealing, turn up one card from the pack. The suit of this card is the highest suit or trumps for the round.
3. The dealer now asks players to predict how many tricks they will win. This is done on the basis of the number of high cards the players have.
4. When the other players have made their bids, the dealer puts in a bid. However his or her bid is dependent on the number of tricks the other players predict they will win. In each round the number of bids must not equal the number of tricks it is possible to get in that round (for example, if no-one predicts they will win in the first round the dealer must also bid zero).
5. Next, starting at the dealer's left, all players put down one card. The highest card wins or takes the "trick".
6. In each round score 10 points for each correct prediction and one point for each trick won.
7. The player with the highest score wins.

Car games

Many games can be played to break up the monotony of a car journey. These are the ones we have enjoyed most.

Unless noted otherwise, they are suitable for players six years and older. You don't need any equipment. Two is the minimum number of players.

If you wish to avoid hectic competitiveness, stick to I spy or Sweepstakes, which are usually quite peaceful games.

Now

This is a game for everyone but the driver and those who suffer from travel sickness.

Pick an object or landmark that can be seen in the distance. All players close their eyes and call out, "Now" when they think the car is passing the goal. The winner is the player whose guess is closest to the goal.

Daddy's list

Equipment: a Daddy with a good memory!

In this game the players look for things around them chosen by a leader. As soon as the first object has been spotted, the players ask what is next (the listmaker need be only a couple of moves ahead), and so on. If someone thinks the thing to find is too hard, they can elect to find *two* of the second item on the list. If another player wants to start looking for the second item on the list they must hunt for *three* of whatever it is, and the next person, *four*. Once a player has said he or she will go on, he or she cannot go back. Of course, if the players find each item in its correct order they have to spot only *one* of each.

I spy

Age 7–12

This is a very well-known car game, but it is a classic for keeping children occupied on long journeys.

One player starts the game by choosing an object on view in the car or outside and saying, "I spy with my little eye something beginning with "g" — or "a", "b", "c" and so on. The player who guesses the correct answer chooses the next object and starts the next round.

Age 4 or 5–9

For younger children make the game more specific, perhaps by stating the colour of the object.

Figures to find

Each player chooses a number between zero and nine. The object of the game is to spot the chosen number on the registration plates of cars that pass. The winner is the player who is the first to spot 10 cars bearing the chosen number. Go on to see who can collect 10 cars with their number appearing twice.

Up to nine

Equipment: pencils and paper are useful

Claim cars in turn as they pass. Each player must look for consecutive numbers from zero to nine then back to zero in the number plates of their chosen cars. Make the game more difficult by looking for a sequence of numbers, such as 123, 678, or 543.

Sides of the road

1. Animal safari: If there are more than two players, split into teams, one for each side of the road. The object of the game is to count the highest number of different types of animals you pass. Decide whether varieties of birds will count before you begin. Choose a point on the route to mark the end of the round — a district boundary, a junction or perhaps the fourth bridge crossed.

2. Town safari: When passing through a town, count up something else mutually decided (for example, two-storeyed buildings, parked cars or people wearing hats). Remember to count what you see on one side of the road only.

Sweepstakes

Set a subject or ask the players to think of something they are likely to pass before reaching the next town. It could be horses, tractors, trucks or anything they enjoy watching out for. The object of the game is to guess the number of times it will be passed. The winner is the player with the closest guess.

I spy the alphabet

This is a variation of the above game, in which each player chooses 25 or 26 objects in turn, beginning with each different letter of the alphabet. (For example, *a*pple tree, *b*arn, *c*aravan and so on.) It is probably wise to omit "q", unless there are quails, quarries or quadrupeds in the area! Adjectives must not be used. Each player chooses different items beginning with each consecutive letter of the alphabet. Older children could help younger ones with this game.

ABC

Split the players into two teams, one for each side of the road, or claim oncoming cars in turn. The object of the game is to find the letters of the alphabet in order on road signs or number plates of cars on each team's respective side of the road.

A variation of this game is to look for the letters of your name in order on the number plates of other cars.

Rainbow

Each player picks a plain colour, which can be found on other cars on the road. Count up the number of cars of that colour within a set time limit. Two-tone models and unusually coloured cars (such as maroon, which could be taken as red or purple) don't count.

What's coming towards you?

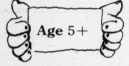
Age 5+

The players look at oncoming cars and, as they pass, claim each one in turn. Who got the Mini? Who got the Mercedes? Of course, the results are totally random, which gives the game its appeal.

If the players are good at identifying makes of cars, turn the game into a guessing game. The winner is the player who first guesses the correct make of the car as it comes closer out of the distance.

First and last

Claim cars in turn as they pass by and add together the first and last numbers on the number plates. The winner is the first player to reach a total of 100. Children younger than six years can also play if they are given a limit of 20 and have to add together only the last number on each car they claim.